ENTREPRENEURSHIP
TEACHING STRATEGIES

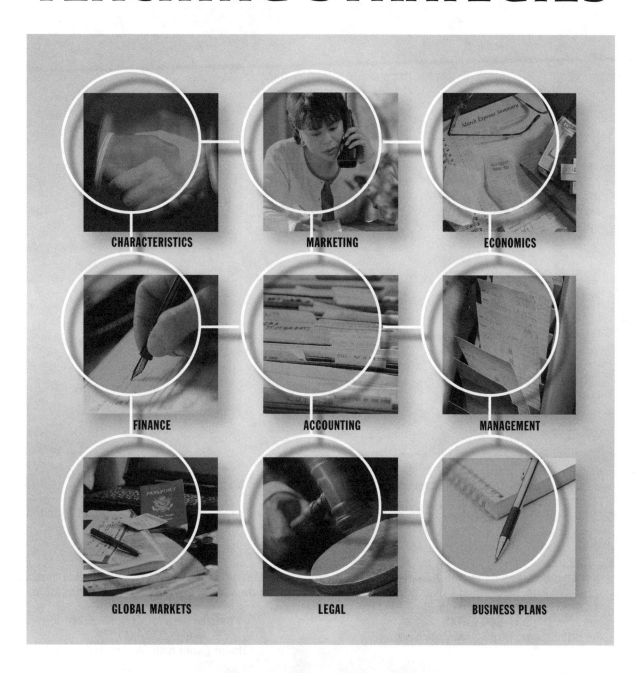

CHARACTERISTICS   MARKETING   ECONOMICS

FINANCE   ACCOUNTING   MANAGEMENT

GLOBAL MARKETS   LEGAL   BUSINESS PLANS

HANDOUTS

John E. Clow, Editor and Project Director

Entrepreneurship Teaching Strategies Handouts

Copyright © 1998 by the National Business Education Association and the Ewing Marion Kauffman Foundation

ISBN 0-933964-52-8

National Business Education Association
1914 Association Drive
Reston, VA 20191-1596
703-860-8300
Home page: http://www.nbea.org

Kauffman Center for Entrepreneurial Leadership
at the Ewing Marion Kauffman Foundation
4900 Oak Street
Kansas City, MO 64112-2776
816-932-1000
Home page: http://www.emkf.org

Any views or recommendations expressed in this book do not necessarily constitute official policy of the National Business Education Association or the Kauffman Center for Entrepreneurial Leadership.

LESSON PLAN I
CHARACTERISTICS

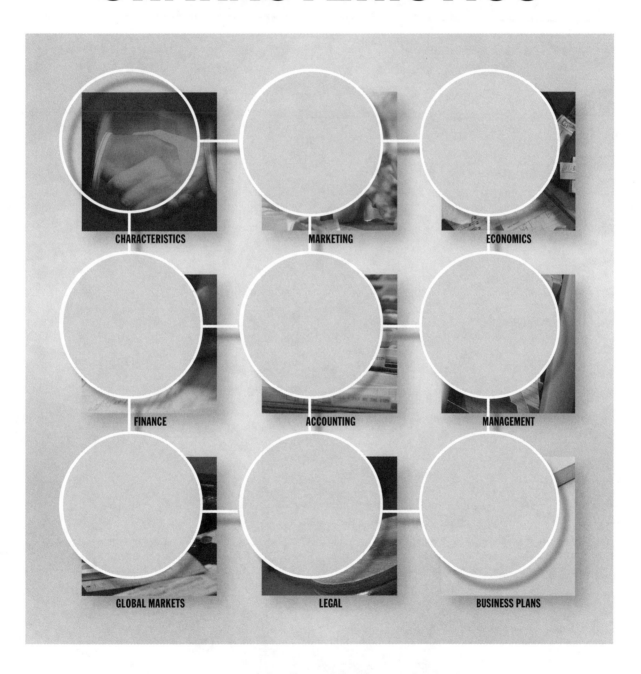

CHARACTERISTICS   MARKETING   ECONOMICS

FINANCE   ACCOUNTING   MANAGEMENT

GLOBAL MARKETS   LEGAL   BUSINESS PLANS

HANDOUTS

Entrepreneur Profile

OBJECTIVE

To understand the entrepreneurial spirit by researching and reporting on an individual who has experienced success in our free enterprise economy.

ASSIGNMENT

Select an individual (living or not) who has been nationally successful in starting and operating his or her own business and write a profile about this person. There are literally thousands of individuals you may use. A few examples are: Wally Amos, Mary Kay Ash, Warren Buffet, Jenny Craig, Bill Gates, John H. Johnson, Calvin Klein, Ray Kroc, Estée Lauder, James Cash Penny, Orville Redenbacher, John D. Rockefeller, Levi Strauss, Sam Walton, etc.

WHAT TO INCLUDE IN THE REPORT

1. Name of the person.

2. Name and description of the company he/she started.

3. Brief history of the individual.

4. An identification of personal characteristics of the individual, such as aptitudes, abilities, skills, and philosophies.

5. Your opinion about why this person was so successful as an entrepreneur rather than as a manager.

6. Visual aid, such as an ad for the company or a picture of individual.

SUGGESTED RESOURCES

Books — use the individual's name as the keyword in your search.

Current Biography — a prominent series that profiles personalities in the news.

Periodicals — magazines such as *Money*, *Forbes*, and *Business Week*.

Your report should be typed using double spacing and written in standard English. Use good organization, appropriate word choice, sentence and paragraph structure, as well as correct punctuation, capitalization, and spelling. Be sure to include bibliography information.

Prepare a brief, two or three minute, oral report for the class about the entrepreneur you researched.

ASSESSMENT

Your final grade will be based on the above criteria as well as the oral presentation.

A Great Entrepreneur

"When I see a barrier, I cry and curse, and then I get a ladder and climb over it."

John H. Johnson

Stories about self-made millionaires who pulled themselves up from poverty and obscurity have always been intriguing, and the one about John H. Johnson is no exception. There probably were not many who believed that this grandson of slaves, born in a shack in the segregated South and growing up during the Great Depression, had a promising future. But Johnson overcame the obstacles of poverty, negativism, and racism to reach great heights in the publishing world and become the first black man to be named to the *Forbes 400 List of Richest Men.*

As a high school student, Johnson walked up to an assembly speaker, who was president of a large black-owned insurance company, introduced himself, and said he wanted to go to college but didn't have the money. The speaker told this gutsy and determined young African-American to come see him in the fall. Johnson did just that, announcing that "he had an appointment" with the company president. This self-confidence and determination earned him a part-time job so that he could attend the University of Chicago.

Johnson continued his studies and job, and within a few years was named editor of the company's in-house magazine, which contained articles on contemporary, successful African-Americans. This experience inspired him to create a magazine for and about black Americans, *Negro Digest.* He recognized that a huge market existed for this product because there was no other national black consumer magazine. He identified that the African-American population had a need for a national magazine that would feature stories from and about successful African-Americans and that advertising targeted to this group would result in huge product sales for the advertiser.

Many individuals told him his idea would not work, but he refused to limit his ambitions. In order to raise the starting capital to print the first issue, he borrowed $500 using his mother's furniture as collateral. He demonstrated his creative side when, to get newsstands to carry his magazine, he paid his friends to go around and ask for the magazine until they carried it. To start the selling process, he paid his friends to buy the magazines.

In 1945, Johnson printed his first edition of *Ebony,* which caused him to become a major force in the publishing world. He continued to add other magazines (including *Jet* and *Ebony Jr.*), a cosmetics company, an insurance company, radio stations, and real estate holdings. In the 1990s, his magazines have a combined circulation of 2.5 million, and he has become known as "perhaps the richest and certainly the most powerful African-American businessman in the country."

REFERENCES

Gross, Daniel and the editors of *Forbes* Magazine. (1996). *Forbes Greatest Business Stories of All Time.* Wiley and Sons.

Pile, Robert B. (1993). *Top Entrepreneurs and Their Businesses.* Oliver Press.

Test Your Entrepreneurial Quotient (EQ)

INSTRUCTIONS

Read the following questions and respond using the numbers to the right of the question.

	Never	Seldom	Usually	Always
1. Typing up a report, which is due tomorrow, has kept you up until the early morning hours. As you start your last paragraph, the computer crashes and the report is gone. Would you stay up for the rest of the night to do it over?	1	2	3	4
2. Your class needs to raise money for an exciting field trip. Are you the one who thinks of ways to earn the money?	1	2	3	4
3. At a baseball game, it is the bottom of the eighth inning and your team trails 5 - 0. People begin leaving to avoid traffic. Do you stay and cheer even louder?	1	2	3	4
4. Do you keep track of assignments, scheduled activities, and other time commitments in some sort of organizer?	1	2	3	4
5. When given an assignment due in one month, some people wait three weeks to even begin. Do you start the assignment right away?	1	2	3	4
6. Are you willing to try new foods, travel to new places, and meet new people?	1	2	3	4
7. When working on a group project, do you freely express your ideas even if they seem unpopular?	1	2	3	4
8. If an activity interests you, are you genuinely happy about working very hard at it?	1	2	3	4
9. For your summer job, the company has offered you $8.00 per hour or minimum wage plus commission. Do you accept the commission offer?	1	2	3	4
10. On their concert tour, your favorite musicians have scheduled a stop in your town. Unfortunately, tickets are sold out. Would you continue to try to find other ways of getting a ticket?	1	2	3	4
Total EQ Score (add scores from questions 1 through 10): _____				

What do the results of this EQ Test suggest about your personality?

Entrepreneurial Quotient (EQ) Test Results

INSTRUCTIONS

Use these criteria to compare your EQ Test score with the personality profile of a "typical" entrepreneur.

Range	Tendencies	Summary of Results
32 - 40	High	Look out Bill Gates! You have very strong entrepreneurial qualities.
24 - 31	Above Average	Hey, this might be for you! Identify your lower scoring areas and make a consistent, conscious effort to develop more positive behaviors in those areas.
16 - 23	Average	You have entrepreneurial potential. Carefully examine your desire to be your own boss. If your desire is high, commit yourself to strengthening these characteristics. Use the profiles from this lesson as inspiration.
15 and Less	Below Average	Your success will be greater in management or support opportunities.

EQ Test Responses/Discussion. (Important characteristics of entrepreneurs are **bold** in each answer.)

1. When the going gets tough, entrepreneurs get tougher! They possess **determination** to accomplish tasks in spite of obstacles.

2. Entrepreneurs are **creative**, "idea people."

3. Entrepreneurs **don't give up easily**. Their drive keeps them from quitting because they believe in themselves and their ideas.

4. Although systems differ, you'll rarely find a successful entrepreneur without **organizational skills** to keep track of the details.

5. Entrepreneurs don't waste time. They tackle even undesirable tasks with **discipline** and **self-motivation**.

6. **Curiosity** and **willingness to take calculated risks** are hallmarks of an entrepreneurial spirit.

7. **Self-assuredness** and **confidence** — a deep belief in themselves — are common threads among entrepreneurs.

8. Others tire just watching the **hard work** and **energy level** of entrepreneurs.

9. Never content with "good enough," the **self-confidence** and **desire** of entrepreneurs drive them to accept opportunities for greater success.

10. Knowing there's more than one way to reach a goal, entrepreneurs are very **resourceful**.

Charlie's Chance for Change

Charlie is at a major crossroads in her life. Her daily ritual, as it has been for the past 20 years, begins at 6:00 a.m. She promptly meets her car pool at 7:00 a.m. and works hard from 8:00 a.m. to 5:00 p.m. Charlie is an aerospace engineer at Cohen, a design and manufacturing company. Cohen's largest contract is with the U.S. government to produce military aircraft.

Now, as a result of huge defense spending cutbacks, Cohen must downsize to stay in business. For long-term employees like Charlie, Cohen has offered a "golden handshake" — monetary compensation for taking an early retirement. The package Charlie is taking is the equivalent of the salary she would earn for two years of service.

So, at age 44, Charlie has decided to use this money to fulfill her long desire to become her own boss. After reading more about Charlie and her community, your task is to identify entrepreneurial opportunities that seem well-suited for her.

ABOUT CHARLIE

Charlie is from a large family which lives in a rural area of the Midwest. She earned her weekly allowance by caring for the dozens of animals on their property. She loved them all — dogs, cats, pigs, horses, goats, hamsters, birds, and rabbits. Sometimes, as she was feeding the animals, her mind wandered to distant places as she watched the planes fly overhead. She often thought how wonderful it must be to visit all the exciting places she read about.

A small portion of Charlie's allowance was saved for a purchase at the local music store. Although rock was her favorite, she enjoyed listening to a variety of music and spent most of her money on expanding her music collection. In her free time,

Charlie enjoyed creating toys out of wood scraps for her younger siblings.

As she began to plan for her high school graduation, Charlie considered careers in the music or travel industries, but her conservative Midwestern family convinced her to pursue a more "stable" field. As a result, she earned her engineering degree and moved to the West Coast.

Charlie's home now is full of animals, stereo equipment, and a large assortment of wooden toys she created for her own children. Now that her children are away at college, she and her husband travel on their vacations throughout the world.

While at Cohen, much of Charlie's engineering work involved extensive research. As a result, she is creative and has excellent oral and written communication skills. She is very knowledgeable about computers, including how to use a variety of software, as well as how to repair and build computers.

ABOUT LOGAN HILLS

Logan Hills is referred to as a "bedroom community," meaning most of the employed residents commute almost an hour each way to their jobs in the city. Housing is affordable, pollution is almost nonexistent, and the crime rate is low, which is why people are willing to make the long drive each day.

Like many places where the population has grown rapidly, business and industry growth is far behind residential growth. There are plans for a regional shopping mall, an autoplex, and a 15-screen movie theater, but for now, the stores and restaurants are all in small strip centers throughout the town. Only a few professional services

Characteristics Handout I-B-1

exist in the community, so residents mostly use business services in the metropolitan area.

Using the information below, give Charlie your suggestions for her entrepreneurial venture. Describe the type of business she should start and the rationale for your suggestions. Then briefly describe the steps she should take in establishing her business.

Educational Attainment (Persons 25 and Over)		
Less than 9th grade	304	1%
Less than 12th grade	1,010	4%
High School Graduate	6,296	25%
Associate's Degree	8,207	33%
Bachelor's Degree	9,563	34%

Population by Age		
13 and under	4,380	12%
14 - 24	6,935	19%
25 - 39	9,490	26%
40 - 54	6,205	17%
55 - 69	2,190	6%
70 and over	7,300	20%

Workers Per Household		
None	1,703	21%
One	1,460	11%
Two	4,786	59%
Three or more	162	2%

Gender Breakdown	
Male	48%
Female	54%

Household Income		
Less than $ 9,999	324	12%
$10,000 - $19,999	1,136	19%
$20,000 - $34,999	2,190	26%
$35,000 - $49,999	2,839	17%
$50,000 - $74,999	973	6%
$75,000 and over	649	20%

The Book Factory

INSTRUCTIONS

Read the following questions and respond using the numbers to the right of the question.

	Sample	Round 1	Round 2	Round 3	Round 4	Round 5
1. Number of books produced	4					
2. Cost of materials (.50 per book)	$2.00					
3. Number of workers	4					
4. Wages ($2.00 per worker)	$8.00					
5. $4.00 rent for factory desks	$4.00					
6. Investment capital goods ($1.00 per pen)	$1.00					
7. Total costs (add lines 2, 4, 5, and 6)	$15.00					
8. Cost per book (line 7 divided by line 1)	$3.75					
9. Total time worked (5 minutes multiplied by number of workers from line 3)	20 min.					
10. Output per minute worked (number of books divided by total number of minutes — line 1 divided by line 9)	4/20=.20					

LESSON PLAN II
MARKETING

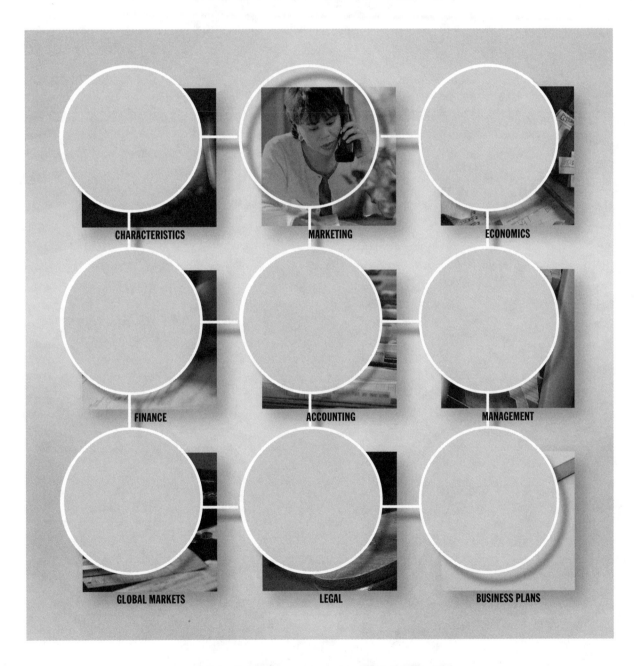

CHARACTERISTICS   MARKETING   ECONOMICS

FINANCE   ACCOUNTING   MANAGEMENT

GLOBAL MARKETS   LEGAL   BUSINESS PLANS

HANDOUTS

Calculating Market Share

INSTRUCTIONS

From the information presented below, calculate market share as a:
- Percentage of units sold.
- Percentage of total revenue.

You have completed a survey of your class members concerning their consumption of candy last week. When you tally the responses, you find that class members purchased 30 Milky Way candy bars, 10 Kit Kat candy bars, 10 Snickers candy bars, and 20 Pay Day candy bars. After checking a local grocery store, you find that the current retail price of each candy bar is as follows:

Milky Way	50 cents
Kit Kat	50 cents
Snickers	60 cents
Pay Day	40 cents

Complete the following table, determining market share for each candy bar.

Candy Bar	Units Sold	Unit Price	Market Share as a Percentage of Unit Sales	Total Revenue Dollars	Market Share as a Percentage of Revenue
Milky Way					
Kit Kat					
Snickers					
Pay Day					
Totals		XXXXXX	100%		100%

Calculating Market Share (Answer Key)

INSTRUCTIONS

From the information presented below, calculate market share as a:
- Percentage of units sold.
- Percentage of total revenue.

You have completed a survey of your class members concerning their consumption of candy last week. When you tally the responses, you find that class members purchased 30 Milky Way candy bars, 10 Kit Kat candy bars, 10 Snickers candy bars, and 20 Pay Day candy bars. After checking a local grocery store, you find that the current retail price of each candy bar is as follows:

Milky Way .... 50 cents
Kit Kat .... 50 cents
Snickers .... 60 cents
Pay Day .... 40 cents

Complete the following table, determining market share for each candy bar.

Candy Bar	Units Sold	Unit Price	Market Share as a Percentage of Unit Sales	Total Revenue Dollars	Market Share as a Percentage of Revenue
Milky Way	30	.50	43%	$15.00	44%
Kit Kat	10	.50	14%	$ 5.00	15%
Snickers	10	.60	14%	$ 6.00	18%
Pay Day	20	.40	29%	$ 8.00	23%
Totals	70	XXXXXX	100%	$34.00	100%

Estimating Market Share of Existing Businesses

INSTRUCTIONS

Select one of the product categories listed below or have another category approved by your instructor. Identify the main competitors in each product category. Locate sales data for the entire industry as well as for each competitor that you identified. Calculate market share for each of the competitors.

Identify the product category that you have selected from the list below:
- ❑ Computers
- ❑ Jeans
- ❑ Soft drinks
- ❑ Athletic shoes
- ❑ Bicycles
- ❑ Other _____

What are total yearly sales for this product category? _____

What was the source of this information?

_____

In the table below, list the main competitors that you have identified in the first column. In the second column, provide the sales data that you have located. Provide the source of that information in the third column. Calculate market share for each competitor, and record that information in the fourth column. You may have to add an "All Others" category.

Competitors	Sales	Source of Information	Market Share

Calculating Market Share — More Practice

INSTRUCTIONS

From the information presented below, calculate market share as a:
- Percentage of units sold.
- Percentage of total revenue.

You have completed a survey of your class members concerning the number of pairs as well as the brand of jeans they purchased during the last six months. When you tally the responses, you find that class members purchased 20 pairs of Levi jeans, 10 pairs of Wrangler jeans, 10 pairs of Guess jeans, and 20 pairs of Gap jeans. After checking local stores, you find that the current retail price of each brand of jeans is as follows:

Levi	$24.99
Wrangler	$24.99
Guess	$44.95
Gap	$35.99

Complete the following table, determining market share for each brand of jeans.

Manufacturer	Units Sold	Unit Price	Market Share as a Percentage of Unit Sales	Total Revenue Dollars	Market Share as a Percentage of Revenue
Levi					
Wrangler					
Guess					
Gap					
Totals		XXXXXX	100%		100%

Calculating Market Share — More Practice (Answer Key)

INSTRUCTIONS

From the information presented below, calculate market share as a:
- Percentage of units sold.
- Percentage of total revenue.

You have completed a survey of your class members concerning the number of pairs as well as the brand of jeans they purchased during the last six months. When you tally the responses, you find that class members purchased 20 pairs of Levi jeans, 10 pairs of Wrangler jeans, 10 pairs of Guess jeans, and 20 pairs of Gap jeans. After checking local stores, you find that the current retail price of each brand of jeans is as follows:

Levi $24.99
Wrangler $24.99
Guess $44.95
Gap $35.99

Complete the following table, determining market share for each brand of jeans.

Manufacturer	Units Sold	Unit Price	Market Share as a Percentage of Unit Sales	Total Revenue Dollars	Market Share as a Percentage of Revenue
Levi	20	$24.99	33%	$ 499.80	26%
Wrangler	10	$24.99	17%	$ 249.90	13%
Guess	10	$44.95	17%	$ 499.50	23%
Gap	20	$35.99	33%	$ 719.80	38%
Totals	60	XXXXXX	100%	$1919.00	100%

Market Segmentation Techniques

INSTRUCTIONS

Obtain a copy of one magazine from your instructor. Your task is to use the market segmentation strategies that we have discussed in class. In a small group, respond to the questions listed below. Refer to specific articles or advertisements that will support your responses. Prepare a report of your findings that you will present to the class. Develop a customer profile that your group feels is the market segment to which this magazine primarily appeals. Prepare visual aids that will support your findings.

DEMOGRAPHIC SEGMENTATION

1. What age group(s) does this magazine appeal to?

   _____

2. What gender does this magazine appeal to?

   _____

3. What educational background do the readers seem to have?

   _____

4. Does the magazine appeal to specific ethnic groups? If so, which ones?

   _____

5. To what income levels does this magazine have primary appeal?

   _____

GEOGRAPHIC SEGMENTATION

1. What is the geographic appeal of this magazine?

   _____

2. Would certain regions of the country be more likely to read this magazine? Explain.

   _____

   _____

   _____

PSYCHOGRAPHIC SEGMENTATION

1. Describe typical lifestyles of people who read this magazine.

   _____

   _____

   _____

2. Describe typical attitudes and opinions of people who read this magazine.

   _____

   _____

   _____

Using Marketing Segmentation to Develop the Framework of a Basic Marketing Plan

INSTRUCTIONS

Divide into groups of three to four students. Respond to questions listed below.

PART 1

1. Develop a short questionnaire to use in surveying students at your school. Questions should focus on collecting demographic (age, gender, ethnic background, family income, etc.), psychographic (use of free time, recreation activities, etc.), and geographic (zip codes, neighborhoods, streets, etc.) information about the student body.

2. Survey 25 students at the school and tally the results of the questionnaire.

3. Identify market segments at the school based on the information that you have collected.

4. In a written report, present the information that you have collected. Illustrate your findings with graphs where appropriate. Based on your findings, identify characteristics of the typical student at your school.

PART 2

1. Identify one business that sells products which would appeal to a market segment that you have identified at your school.

2. Develop the framework of a marketing plan for this business. In a written report identify:
   A. Specific products that would be sold by this business.
   B. Suggested retail prices for these products.
   C. Promotion strategies that this business could use.
   D. A site in the community where this business could be located.

You will be evaluated on how well your marketing plan focuses on the market segment that you have identified at your school.

Customer Loyalty Programs

INSTRUCTIONS

You will be assigned to a business in the community that implements a customer loyalty program. Arrange to interview the manager of that firm and answer the following questions. Be prepared to present your findings to the class.

Name of Business

_____

Business Address

_____

Telephone Number

_____

Manager's Name

_____

1. Describe the program or activities used by the business to generate customer loyalty.

   _____

   _____

   _____

2. How is the customer loyalty program promoted to customers?

   _____

   _____

   _____

3. How long has the customer loyalty program been in effect? When is the program scheduled to end?

   _____

   _____

   _____

4. Approximately what percent of customers take advantage of the program?

   _____

   _____

   _____

5. Describe any extra administrative activities required by implementing the customer loyalty program.

   _____

   _____

   _____

6. Estimate the costs involved by providing the customer loyalty program.

   _____

   _____

   _____

What Do Customers Think?

SITUATION

John Anderson, owner of John's Music Store, has been faced with declining sales over the past four months. He doesn't know what is causing the problem. Over the years, his customers have been extremely loyal to the store. To build and reward customer loyalty, John has implemented a customer loyalty program that gives customers a free CD after they have purchased 20.

John is interested in finding out information from current customers that might be beneficial in designing strategies that could be used to increase sales. As a sales associate in the store, you have been asked to design questions that the owner could use on a survey that he plans to distribute to current customers.

John has asked you to submit the form below to him before the end of the day. In the first column, write the questions that you feel should be part of the survey. In the second column, describe how the information collected from the question could be used to develop strategies for increasing sales.

Questions for Survey	How Will This Information Be Used to Develop Strategies?
1. Example At which store do you most often purchase CDs?	1. Example It will identify which store is most popular. Knowing this, John can identify marketing strategies being used there and possibly alter his own strategies.
2.	2.
3.	3.
4.	4.
5.	5.

LESSON PLAN III
ECONOMICS

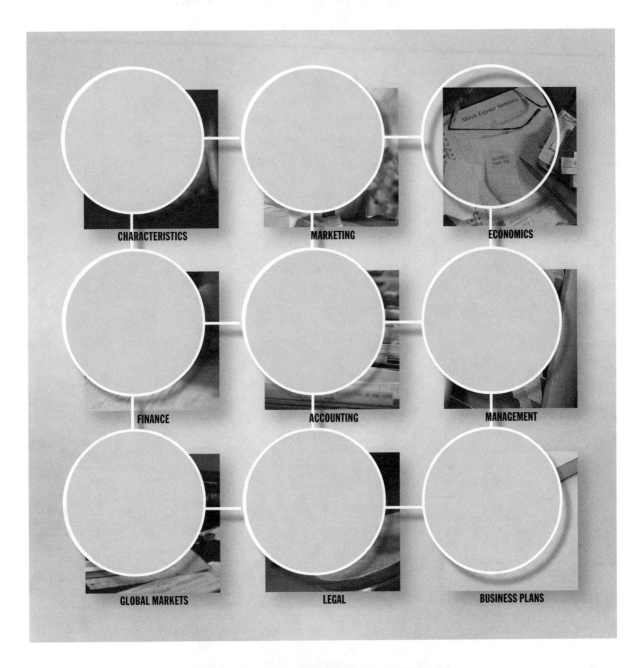

CHARACTERISTICS

MARKETING

ECONOMICS

March Expense Summary

FINANCE

ACCOUNTING

MANAGEMENT

GLOBAL MARKETS

LEGAL

BUSINESS PLANS

HANDOUTS

Terms and Definitions

Market structure is determined by the level (degree) of competition present in the market. While there are variations, it is generally agreed that there are several types of markets including: monopoly, oligopoly, cartel, monopolistic competitve, and pure competition. The characteristics of each are identified below.

MONOPOLY

- One seller
- No competition except substitute goods
- Considerable latitude in setting price

OLIGOPOLY

- Few sellers of an identical good
- Some competition but relatively low level
- Informal collusion occurs as sellers deal in markets

CARTEL

- Few sellers
- Similar to oligopoly and monopoly
- Collusion enables few sellers to act like a monopoly since they set the price

MONOPOLISTIC COMPETITION

- Many sellers
- Differentiated product, close to identical
- Advertising/promotion creates impression that supplier is the only place to secure item

PURE COMPETITION

- Many sellers
- So many sellers, no single seller or group can fix or affect price appreciably
- Interaction of buyers and sellers in marketplace set the price
- Identical or very similar product

Willard's Hardware Store

INSTRUCTIONS

Now that you have some understanding about different types of market structures, let's see how an individual running a small business would use this information. Read the following case problems and answer the questions listed below.

Willard wants to start a hardware store in his small community. The closest hardware stores are about 25 miles away in a larger community. In that larger community, there are approximately 10 hardware stores. Many residents who live in Willard's town work in the larger community. He discovers there are few hardware producers who will sell to him because his orders are so small.

1. What kind of market structure does he encounter as a seller? Support your answer.

_____

_____

_____

_____

2. What kind of market structure does he encounter as a buyer?

_____

_____

_____

_____

_____

3. What degree of freedom does Willard have in negotiating prices with his suppliers? What degree of freedom does Willard have in setting his prices for selling products to customers?

_____

_____

_____

_____

_____

Willard's Hardware Store (Answer Key)

INSTRUCTIONS

Now that you have some understanding about different types of market structures, let's see how an individual running a small business would use this information. Read the following case problems and answer the questions listed below.

Willard wants to start a hardware store in his small community. The closest hardware stores are about 25 miles away in a larger community. In that larger community, there are approximately 10 hardware stores. Many residents who live in Willard's town work in the larger community. He discovers there are few hardware producers who will sell to him because his orders are so small.

1. What kind of market structure does he encounter as a seller? Support your answer.

   It may appear that Willard is in a monopolistic market since his is the only hardware store in town. Many residents, however, work in the larger community and can shop at any of the 10 hardware stores during their lunch break or after work. Also, some of the hardware suppliers are probably part of a megastore that offers groceries, banking, and other services/products to its customers. Actually, Willard is in a rather competitive market.

2. What kind of market structure does he encounter as a buyer?

   It appears to be primarily oligopolistic since there are very few suppliers who will deal with Willard.

3. What degree of freedom does Willard have in negotiating prices with his suppliers? What degree of freedom does Willard have in setting his prices for selling products to customers?

   When dealing with his suppliers, Willard has little negotiating power because there are very few suppliers that will work with him because of the size of his shop. In selling products to his customers, Willard will have little freedom because he has to keep his price competitive with the other general hardware stores. Willard might be able to charge more for his products if he differentiated his products from his competitors, such as offering "designer" hardware.

Willard's Dilemma

INSTRUCTIONS

Read the following scenario and answer the questions listed below.

Willard runs into his friend, Valerie, while she is shopping in his hardware store. They begin talking, and Willard discovers Valerie is visiting all the hardware stores to find antique hardware pieces, such as locks, keys, door hinges, door stops, door knockers, etc. These pieces are relatively inexpensive because they are considered "junk" to many of the current hardware store owners.

Valerie is cleaning out the hardware stores' old stock. She is selling the parts for scrap and is getting paid for the metal content of the parts. She also believes there is a market for selling antique hardware pieces. Her belief is based on the fact that reproductions of hardware pieces are selling well. "If reproductions are selling, then why wouldn't there be a market for the actual hardware pieces?" asks Valerie. She doesn't know of anyone in the state who is marketing antique hardware as a business.

1. If Willard follows this avenue for the establishment of his business, what kind of market would he encounter as a seller?

   _____

   _____

   _____

   _____

2. What kind of market would he confront as a buyer?

   _____

   _____

   _____

   _____

   _____

3. Would you say that Willard would have a lot of freedom in setting the price as a seller if there were considerable consumer demand? How much freedom would he have to negotiate a price with his supplier if he was the only buyer of the hardware for other than scrap value?

   _____

   _____

   _____

   _____

4. Why should entrepreneurs understand the structure of the markets in which they operate?

   _____

   _____

   _____

   _____

Willard's Dilemma (Answer Key)

INSTRUCTIONS

Read the following scenario and answer the questions listed below.

Willard runs into his friend, Valerie, while she is shopping in his hardware store. They begin talking, and Willard discovers Valerie is visiting all the hardware stores to find antique hardware pieces, such as locks, keys, door hinges, door stops, door knockers, etc. These pieces are relatively inexpensive because they are considered "junk" to many of the current hardware store owners.

Valerie is cleaning out the hardware stores' old stock. She is selling the parts for scrap and is getting paid for the metal content of the parts. She also believes there is a market for selling antique hardware pieces. Her belief is based on the fact that reproductions of hardware pieces are selling well. "If reproductions are selling, then why wouldn't there be a market for the actual hardware pieces?" asks Valerie. She doesn't know of anyone in the state who is marketing antique hardware as a business.

1. If Willard follows this avenue for the establishment of his business, what kind of market would he encounter as a seller?

   This would be monopolistic if he is the only individual for "miles around" who supplies real antique hardware pieces. It may also be oligopolistic if there are only a few other suppliers of like items, or it could be monopolistic competitive when compared to those selling reproductions of old hardware.

2. What kind of market would he confront as a buyer?

   Again, this would tend to be monopolistic or oligopolistic since there seems to be few individuals at the present time who are buying the old antique hardware.

3. Would you say that Willard would have a lot of freedom in setting the price as a seller if there were considerable consumer demand? How much freedom would he have to negotiate a price with his supplier if he was the only buyer of the hardware for other than scrap value?

   Willard would have a lot of freedom to set the price if his products are in demand because he is one of a few sellers, or can easily differentiate his product from those who sell reproduction hardware. He would have to research what other vendors charge for antique reproductions, but his product would probably be perceived as a very different reproduction. Valerie, as a seller, is in a monopolistic structure as well. Her flexibility, however, would be limited if Willard is her only "good for resale" buyer.

4. Why should entrepreneurs understand the structure of the markets in which they operate?

   Understanding the type of market entrepreneurs operate in is critical to their success because it impacts such crucial decisions as determining the prices to pay/charge for goods and services.

Cost Analysis Sheet for Kites

Amount of Kites Produced	Total Fixed Costs	Total Variable Costs	Marginal Costs	Total Costs	Average Costs
0	$3.00	0	0	$3.00	–
1	$3.00	$ .50	$ .50	$3.50	$3.50
2	$3.00	$ .90	$ .40	$3.90	$1.95
3	$3.00	$1.20	$ .30	$4.20	$1.40
4	$3.00	$1.40	$ .20	$4.40	$1.10
5	$3.00	$1.60	$ .20	$4.60	$ .92
6	$3.00	$1.80	$ .20	$4.80	$ .80

Cost Analysis Sheet for Peanut Butter Sandwiches

Output of Peanut Butter Sandwiches	Total Fixed Costs	Total Variable Costs	Marginal Costs	Total Costs	Average Costs
0	$3.00	0		$3.00	–
1	$3.00	–		–	–
2	$3.00	–		–	–
3	$3.00	–		–	–

True or False?

Answer the following true or false questions.

1. Rent and insurance payments are examples of fixed costs.

   _____

2. The salaries of production workers are a variable cost.

   _____

3. Variable cost is equal to zero if output is equal to zero.

   _____

4. Marginal cost is equal to variable cost.

   _____

5. Raw materials are part of overhead.

   _____

6. An entrepreneur does not need to watch fixed costs.

   _____

7. Fixed costs increase as output increases.

   _____

8. Variable costs can be avoided by producing nothing.

   _____

True or False? (Answer Key)

Answer the following true or false questions.

1. Rent and insurance payments are examples of fixed costs.

   True

2. The salaries of production workers are a variable cost.

   True

3. Variable cost is equal to zero if output is equal to zero.

   True

4. Marginal cost is equal to variable cost.

   False

5. Raw materials are part of overhead.

   False

6. An entrepreneur does not need to watch fixed costs.

   False

7. Fixed costs increase as output increases.

   False

8. Variable costs can be avoided by producing nothing.

   True

Case Studies

1. Larry's Grocery Store carries specialty groceries in a downtown area. It has quite limited floor space but Larry decides to add more merchandise. This means that the shelves will be more crowded since he is not adding any more space. What will happen to the fixed costs of the operation, the variable costs, and the average costs, for the existing items?

   Fixed costs remain the same unless he adds more insurance coverage because of the value of the new items, variable costs increase because of the cost of the new items, average costs for the existing items decrease because fixed costs are spread over more items.

2. Sally runs a cookie baking business out of her home. She decides to put in a new oven, which is larger than her old one and has a process taking less time to bake the cookies. What will happen to fixed costs, variable costs, average costs, and marginal costs if she puts in the new oven and starts production?

   Generally, those fixed costs will increase initially because of buying the new oven, which would cost more than the old one. Variable costs could increase because more raw materials would be needed to produce more cookies. As she gains additional experience working with the oven, the marginal costs of producing the additional batches of cookies would decrease because of more efficient production and cheaper raw materials from buying in greater volume. Average costs of batches would decrease because of lower fixed costs per unit and lower marginal costs, up to a point.

Government OKs Slower Deployment for Air Bags

INSTRUCTIONS

Read the following article, "Government OKs Slower Deployment for Air Bags," from the March 15, 1997 edition of *The Washington Post* and answer the questions listed below.

WASHINGTON — The government gave auto companies permission Friday to reduce the deployment speeds of air bags to protect children, even though it could put some large adults at greater risk.

Because of the rule by the National Highway Traffic Safety Administration, automakers will begin installing slower bags late in the 1997 model year. Some auto companies said consumers might be able to retrofit existing cars, but could not estimate what it would cost.

The action comes in the wake of a public outcry over deaths caused by air bags, which inflate at speeds of up to 200 mph. The new rule will lower the top deployment speed to 160 mph. Many air bags will inflate at even lower speeds.

Air bags have saved the lives of at least 1,750 drivers and passengers over the last decade, the safety administration said. But the bags have been blamed for the deaths of 38 children, none older than nine, and 24 adults.

Nearly all of the victims were unbelted or out of position — improperly belted or sitting too close to the air bag — factors that federal and industry safety officials said contributed significantly to the deaths.

Most of the children who were killed also were in the front passenger seat. Safety officials say children younger than 12 should never be allowed to sit in the front of a car.

The air bags now on the market deploy with so much force because they were designed to protect the "average unbelted adult," which the safety administration had defined as an adult male who is 5-feet 9-inches tall and weighs 165 pounds. Smaller adults, especially women, and small children are more vulnerable to the impact.

Government and industry officials conceded Friday that the slower deploying air bags might put large unbelted adults at greater risk of death or serious injury in crashes.

"But we're willing to accept that trade-off on an interim basis in the interest of protecting the lives of children and smaller adults," said Philip Recht, deputy administrator of the safety administration.

The safety administration said children deserved priority because they are "less mature than teenagers and adults and thus less able to exercise independent judgement" to protect themselves.

"The government will attempt to limit the risk to adults by boosting its efforts to get more people to wear seat belts," Recht said.

The government and industry also will continue efforts to develop air bags capable of inflating at a speed appropriate to the weight and position of passengers. These "smart" air bags are supposed to come on the market late in 2001.

Earlier this year, the safety administration authorized car companies to install switches that allow vehicle owners to turn air bags on and off.

The safety administration said Friday it is continuing to study the idea of allowing owners of cars with the current generation of air bags to permanently disconnect the safety devices. Under existing rules, air bags can be permanently disconnected for medical reasons, but only with specific approval from the safety administration.

© 1997, *The Washington Post*. Reprinted with permission.

1. What action related to air bags for automobiles is discussed in the article?

2. What is the major benefit of automobile air bags? What is the cost to the individual consumer of the air bags?

3. How many lives have been saved by air bags in the past decade? How many deaths have been blamed on air bags?

4. How has consumer behavior contributed to air bag injuries and deaths?

5. The air bags discussed in the article were designed to protect what group of people who are most vulnerable to injury or death from the air bags?

6. Why do producers make automobiles with air bags to protect "unbelted" adults?

7. Why should all consumers, even those who regularly use seat belts, have to pay more for cars with air bags to protect "unbelted" adults?

8. What trade-offs regarding unbelted adults and children is the federal government willing to make if it allows auto producers to reduce the deployment speed of air bags? Why is it willing to make this trade-off?

_____

_____

_____

_____

9. For what reasons does the government allow automobile owners to permanently disconnect air bags?

_____

_____

_____

10. Why do you think the safety administration authorized car companies to start installing switches that allow vehicle owners to turn air bags on and off? Do you feel this is good or bad? Why?

_____

_____

_____

_____

11. If you were the head of a small business, which produces the higher-powered air bags for the car industry, what would be the effect of this decision?

_____

_____

_____

_____

_____

12. Suppose that a year before this decision was rendered, you heard that this policy may be made soon regarding lower-powered air bags. As the head of a business making the higher-powered air bags, what would you start doing?

_____

_____

_____

_____

_____

Government OKs Slower Deployment for Air Bags (Answer Key)

INSTRUCTIONS

Read the following article, "Government OKs Slower Deployment for Air Bags," from the March 15, 1997 edition of *The Washington Post* and answer the questions listed below.

WASHINGTON — The government gave auto companies permission Friday to reduce the deployment speeds of air bags to protect children, even though it could put some large adults at greater risk.

Because of the rule by the National Highway Traffic Safety Administration, automakers will begin installing slower bags late in the 1997 model year. Some auto companies said consumers might be able to retrofit existing cars, but could not estimate what it would cost.

The action comes in the wake of a public outcry over deaths caused by air bags, which inflate at speeds of up to 200 mph. The new rule will lower the top deployment speed to 160 mph. Many air bags will inflate at even lower speeds.

Air bags have saved the lives of at least 1,750 drivers and passengers over the last decade, the safety administration said. But the bags have been blamed for the deaths of 38 children, none older than nine, and 24 adults.

Nearly all of the victims were unbelted or out of position — improperly belted or sitting too close to the air bag — factors that federal and industry safety officials said contributed significantly to the deaths.

Most of the children who were killed also were in the front passenger seat. Safety officials say children younger than 12 should never be allowed to sit in the front of a car.

The air bags now on the market deploy with so much force because they were designed to protect the "average unbelted adult," which the safety administration had defined as an adult male who is 5-foot-9 and weighs 165 pounds. Smaller adults, especially women, and small children are more vulnerable to the impact.

Government and industry officials conceded Friday that the slower deploying air bags might put large unbelted adults at greater risk of death or serious injury in crashes.

"But we're willing to accept that trade-off on an interim basis in the interest of protecting the lives of children and smaller adults," said Philip Recht, deputy administrator of the safety administration.

The safety administration said children deserved priority because they are "less mature than teenagers and adults and thus less able to exercise independent judgement" to protect themselves.

"The government will attempt to limit the risk to adults by boosting its efforts to get more people to wear seat belts," Recht said.

The government and industry also will continue efforts to develop air bags capable of inflating at a speed appropriate to the weight and position of passengers. These "smart" air bags are supposed to come on the market late in 2001.

Earlier this year, the safety administration authorized car companies to install switches that allow vehicle owners to turn air bags on and off.

The safety administration said Friday it is continuing to study the idea of allowing owners of cars with the current generation of air bags to permanently disconnect the safety devices. Under existing rules, air bags can be permanently disconnected for medical reasons, but only with specific approval from the safety administration.

1. What action related to air bags for automobiles is discussed in the article?

   The government gave automobile companies permission to reduce deployment speeds of air bags.

2. What is the major benefit of automobile air bags? What is the cost to the individual consumer of the air bags?

   The major benefit of air bags is saving lives of drivers and passengers. The air bag component to the automobile is the added cost for the consumer.

3. How many lives have been saved by air bags in the past decade? How many deaths have been blamed on air bags?

   According to the article, there were 1,750 lives saved by air bags and 62 deaths blamed on air bags — 38 children under nine and 24 adults.

4. How has consumer behavior contributed to air bag injuries and deaths?

   Many of those who were killed or injured by air bags were unbelted or out of position, improperly belted, or sitting too close to the air bags. Most of the children who were killed or injured were in the front passenger seat.

5. The air bags discussed in the article were designed to protect what group of people who are most vulnerable to injury or death from the air bags?

   The air bags were designed to protect the "average unbelted adult" — a male who is 5-feet 9-inches tall and weighs 165 pounds.

Small adults, especially women, and small children are most vulnerable.

6. Why do producers make automobiles with air bags to protect "unbelted" adults?

   The federal government required all automobiles produced and sold in the U.S. to be equipped with air bags.

7. Why should all consumers, even those who regularly use seat belts, have to pay more for cars with air bags to protect "unbelted" adults?

   Based on the fact the federal government has passed a law requiring air bags, it appears this is the "will of the majority." Also, those who study automobile safety believe the air bag provides protection in addition to that provided by the use of seat belts.

8. What trade-offs regarding unbelted adults and children is the federal government willing to make if it allows auto producers to reduce the deployment speed of air bags? Why is it willing to make this trade-off?

   The trade-off is that slower deploying air bags may increase the risk of death or serious injury for large unbelted adults but they will decrease the risk for children and smaller adults. It believes children deserve priority because they are "less mature than teenagers and adults and less able to exercise independent judgment" to protect themselves.

9. For what reasons does the government allow automobile owners to permanently disconnect air bags?

   Air bags may be permanently disconnected for medical reasons, with specific approval from the safety administration.

10. Why do you think the safety administration authorized car companies to start installing switches that allow vehicle owners to turn air bags on and off? Do you feel this is good or bad? Why?

Switches will allow smaller adults who are at more risk to more easily disconnect air bags. Responses will vary: This is good

because it allows those who are at more risk to easily disconnect the air bags. It is bad because it defeats the purpose of air bags in autos if drivers routinely switch them off.

11. If you were the head of a small business, which produces the higher-powered air bags for the car industry, what would be the effect of this decision?

Car companies would not want to purchase any more of the higher-powered air bags. Firm would have to change product in order to be in accordance with law necessary for maintaining sales. The primary change would probably be inserting a lower-powered igniter into the air bag package.

12. Suppose that a year before this decision was rendered, you heard that this policy may be made soon regarding lower-powered air bags. As the head of a business making the higher-powered air bags, what would you start doing?

Answers will vary. Some may try to lobby the government to maintain the higher-powered requirement. Some will start working on a new product in case a different ruling is made. Others may indicate they would do nothing. It is important to look at the costs and benefits of each decision.

LESSON PLAN IV
FINANCE

CHARACTERISTICS

MARKETING

ECONOMICS

FINANCE

ACCOUNTING

MANAGEMENT

GLOBAL MARKETS

LEGAL

BUSINESS PLANS

HANDOUTS

Types of Business Expenses

Identify each of the following expenditures listed below as a start-up, operating, or personal expenses.

A. Start-up expense
B. Operating expense
C. Personal expense

1. Opening inventory
   _____

2. Payment on owner's car used for business
   _____

3. Apartment rent
   _____

4. Business license
   _____

5. Advertising for "grand opening"
   _____

6. Electric/gas bill at owner's home
   _____

7. Installation of business telephone
   _____

8. Payroll expenses
   _____

9. Payment on delivery truck used in business
   _____

10. Down payment on delivery truck used in business
    _____

11. Employee salaries
    _____

12. Monthly inventory purchases
    _____

13. Cash register repairs
    _____

14. Utilities deposit
    _____

15. Payroll taxes
    _____

Types of Business Expenses (Answer Key)

INSTRUCTIONS

Identify each of the following expenditures listed below as a start-up, operating, or personal expenses.

A. Start-up expense
B. Operating expense
C. Personal expense

1. Opening inventory

   A [Start-Up Expense]

2. Payment on owner's car used for business

   B [Operating Expense]

3. Apartment rent

   C [Personal Expense]

4. Business license

   A [Start-Up Expense]

5. Advertising for "grand opening"

   A [Start-Up Expense]

6. Electric/gas bill at owner's home

   C [Personal Expense]

7. Installation of business telephone

   A [Start-Up Expense]

8. Payroll expenses

   B [Operating Expense]

9. Payment on delivery truck used in business

   B [Operating Expense]

10. Down payment on delivery truck used in business

    A or B [Start-Up Expense or Operating Expense, if purchased after business has been started]

11. Employee salaries

    B [Operating Expense]

12. Monthly inventory purchases

    B [Operating Expense]

13. Cash register repairs

    B [Operating Expense]

14. Utilities deposit

    A [Start-Up Expense]

15. Payroll taxes

    B [Operating Expense]

Sources of Funds for a Business

For each of the following, identify the benefits and drawbacks to entrepreneurs for using each funding source.

Sources	Benefits	Drawbacks
Using Personal Savings		
Forming a Partnership		
Incorporating the Business		
Finding a Venture Capitalist		
Borrowing From Friends or Family		
Borrowing rrom Commercial Sources (Such as Banks)		
Obtaining Trade Credit		

Sources of Funds for a Business (Answer Key)

INSTRUCTIONS

For each of the following, identify the benefits and drawbacks to entrepreneurs for using each funding source.

Source	Benefits	Drawbacks
Using Personal Savings	• Reduces amount of debt owner needs to incur, and reduces the amount of interest that must be paid • Personal investment increases motivation to succeed • Large personal investment shows owner's confidence to potential lenders	• Loss of return from having savings in interest-bearing accounts • May cause personal sacrifices such as lower standard of living
Forming a Partnership	• Brings in additional sources of capital and expertise • Financial risks are shared	• Personal conflicts may interfere with growth and development of the business • Gives up part of the profits and control
Incorporating the Business	• Larger amounts of cash can be obtained	• Complexity and costs of forming a corporation • Gives up part of ownership
Finding a Venture Capitalist	• Large amounts of money may be available	• Most small businesses do not qualify or meet selective criteria • Gives up part ownership and control
Borrowing From Friends or Family	• Quick source of cash with few restrictions • May not be faced with strictly enforced repayment dates • Maintains ownership and control	• Risk of destroying personal relationships • May encourage unwanted involvement in the business
Borrowing from Commercial Sources (Such as Banks)	• Ability to obtain needed funds without giving up part owner-ship and control of the business	• In some situations, lenders may be conservative in deciding whether to make loan • Interest payments can be high
Obtaining Trade Credit	• Less money needed at the time new business opens • Owner's funds can be used for other parts of the business	• For a new entrepreneur, trade credit may be difficult to obtain without an established credit rating.

How Much Will It Cost Me?

INSTRUCTIONS

Contact the bank or financial institution that you have been assigned. Record responses to these questions in the space provided.

1. Name of bank/financial institution

   _____

   _____

   _____

2. Address

   _____

   _____

   _____

3. Representative contacted

   _____

   _____

4. What are the requirements for obtaining a small business loan?

   _____

   _____

   _____

   _____

5. What is the MINIMUM amount usually provided for small business loans?

   _____

   _____

   _____

6. What is the MAXIMUM amount usually provided for small business loans?

   _____

   _____

   _____

7. What is the current interest rate for a small business loan?

   _____

8. What are typical repayment plans for small business loans?

   _____

   _____

9. For what types of small businesses are loans most often approved?

   _____

   _____

   _____

   _____

   _____

Fixed or Variable Expenses?

INSTRUCTIONS

For each of the following, identify the expense as fixed or variable.

Type of Expense	Fixed	Variable
Business License		
Repairs		
Payroll		
Rent		
Utilities, Such as Gas or Electric		
Insurance Payment on Delivery Truck		
Telephone Installation		
Legal Fees for Partnership Agreement		
Membership Dues to Chamber of Commerce		
Basic Telephone Service		
Supplies		

Fixed or Variable Expenses? (Answer Key)

INSTRUCTIONS

For each of the following, identify the expense as fixed or variable.

Type of Expense	Fixed	Variable
Business License	✓	
Repairs		✓
Payroll		✓
Rent	✓ A portion may be variable if based on a percentage of sales	
Utilities, Such as Gas or Electric		✓
Insurance Payment on Delivery Truck	✓	
Telephone Installation	✓	
Legal Fees for Partnership Agreement	✓	
Membership Dues to Chamber of Commerce	✓	
Basic Telephone Service	✓	
Supplies		✓

Break-Even Point Worksheet

INSTRUCTIONS

Read the following scenario and complete the problems.

Your class is starting a business that constructs and sells small plastic clocks. All the materials that are needed to produce 50 clocks can be purchased in a kit for $135. Currently, this is the smallest size kit available.

Your class purchased one kit. Three students stayed after school one afternoon and assembled the clocks. They were paid $22. In addition, each student will receive a 10% commission on each clock that he or she sells.

One of the first things your class wants to calculate is how many clocks have to be sold before realizing a profit. Class members have agreed upon a retail price of $5 for the clocks.

Before the break-even point can be calculated, expenses must be classified as either fixed or variable. In this situation, the product kit and wages paid to the construction workers are fixed. Commissions on sales are variable.

Like all business owners, you can make "what if" estimations about the profit/loss that will occur at various levels of sales. The following examples show what profit/loss will occur when one clock or five clocks are sold. The first two lines on the table shown in Problem #1 illustrate these two examples.

EXAMPLE #1

If your class sells one clock, Total Revenue (sales dollars) generated would only be $5. However, the kit for the clocks and construction expenses have already been paid. So your class has those expenses no matter how many clocks are sold. In other words, these are fixed expenses. The only variable expense the class has is sales commission. This expense fluctuates up or down with sales. With Total Revenues of $5, the commissions would be only 50 cents. All expenses would total $157.50. Expenses would be subtracted from Total Revenue to determine if a profit or loss occurred. In this situation (when only one clock is sold), your class will have a loss of $152.50.

EXAMPLE 2

What if your class sells 5 clocks? Will you start earning a profit? Total revenue generated would be $25 (5 clocks x $5 each). Again, you still have the $157 in fixed expenses regardless of how many clocks are sold. In this situation, the commissions would be $2.50 (10% of sales revenue). When Total Expenses ($159.50) are subtracted from Total Revenue ($25), a loss of $134.50 would occur.

PROBLEM #1

Complete the remaining blanks on the chart that follows. Determine if a profit or loss occurs at each of the following sales levels: 10, 20, 25, 30, 35, 40, 45, and 50.

Number of Clocks Sold	Total Revenue at That Sale Volume	Fixed Expenses	Variable Expenses	Total Expenses	Profit/ Loss
1	$ 5.00	$157.00	$ .50	$ 157.50	($152.50)
5	$ 25.00	$157.00	$ 2.50	$159.50	($134.50)
10					
20					
25					
30					
35					
40					
45					
50					

By examining the table, determine how many clocks must be sold in order for the class to start making a profit?

_____

The first profit occurs when _____ clocks are sold.

PROBLEM #2

Once your class members examine this break-even point analysis, they realize that even if all the clocks are sold, they will only make $68.00 profit. Class members decide that they need to earn more profit. They do some comparison shopping in some local retail stores and find similar clocks are priced from $9 to $13. After some discussion, the class decides that the retail price of the clocks should be $10 rather than $5. The price of the product kit, construction costs, and commission percentage remain the same as in the previous problem.

Complete the blanks on the chart that follows. Determine what profit/loss occurs at each of the following sales levels: 5, 10, 15, 20, 30, 40, 50. The profit/loss calculation has already been made when only one clock is sold.

Number of Clocks Sold	Total Revenue at That Sale Volume	Fixed Expenses	Variable Expenses	Total Expenses	Profit/ Loss
1	$ 10.00	$157.00	$ 1.00	$158.00	($148.00)
5					
10					
15					
20					
30					
40					
50					

By examining the table, determine how many clocks must be sold in order for the class to start making a profit. (Hint: You may have to do some additional calculations to determine the exact number of clocks that must be sold before your class starts to make a profit.)

The first profit occurs when _____ clocks are sold.

INSTRUCTIONS

Based on problems #1 and #2, answer the following questions

1. Why can't an entrepreneur ordinarily reach the break-even point by selling just a few items?

   _____

   _____

   _____

   _____

   _____

   _____

2. Why did the group in problem #2 reach the break-even point before the group in problem #1?

   _____

   _____

   _____

   _____

   _____

   _____

Break-Even Point Worksheet (Answer Key)

INSTRUCTIONS

Read the following scenario and complete the problems.

Your class is starting a business that constructs and sells small plastic clocks. All the materials that are needed to produce 50 clocks can be purchased in a kit for $135. Currently, this is the smallest size kit available.

Your class purchased one kit. Three students stayed after school one afternoon and assembled the clocks. They were paid $22. In addition, each student will receive a 10% commission on each clock that he or she sells.

One of the first things your class wants to calculate is how many clocks have to be sold before realizing a profit. Class members have agreed upon a retail price of $5 for the clocks.

Before the break-even point can be calculated, expenses must be classified as either fixed or variable. In this situation, the product kit and wages paid to the construction workers are fixed. Commissions on sales are variable.

Like all business owners, you can make "what if" estimations about the profit/loss that will occur at various levels of sales. The following examples show what profit/loss will occur when one clock or five clocks are sold. The first two lines on the table shown in Problem #1 illustrate these two examples.

EXAMPLE #1

If your class sells one clock, Total Revenue (sales dollars) generated would only be $5. However, the kit for the clocks and construction expenses have already been paid. So your class has those expenses no matter how many clocks are sold. In other words, these are fixed expenses. The only variable expense the class has is sales commission. This expense fluctuates up or down with sales. With Total Revenues of $5, the commissions would be only 50 cents. All expenses would total $157.50. Expenses would be subtracted from Total Revenue to determine if a profit or loss occurred. In this situation (when only one clock is sold), your class will have a loss of $152.50.

EXAMPLE 2

What if your class sells 5 clocks? Will you start earning a profit? Total revenue generated would be $25 (5 clocks x $5 each). Again, you still have the $157 in fixed expenses regardless of how many clocks are sold. In this situation, the commissions would be $2.50 (10% of sales revenue). When Total Expenses ($159.50) are subtracted from Total Revenue ($25), a loss of $134.50 would occur.

PROBLEM #1

Complete the remaining blanks on the chart that follows. Determine if a profit or loss occurs at each of the following sales levels: 10, 20, 25, 30, 35, 40, 45, and 50.

Number of Clocks Sold	Total Revenue at That Sale Volume	Fixed Expenses	Variable Expenses	Total Expenses	Profit/ Loss
1	$ 5.00	$157.00	$ .50	$ 157.50	($152.50)
5	$ 25.00	$157.00	$ 2.50	$159.50	($134.50)
10	$ 50.00	$157.00	$ 5.00	$162.00	($112.00)
20	$100.00	$157.00	$10.00	$167.00	($ 67.00)
25	$125.00	$157.00	$12.50	$169.50	($ 44.50)
30	$150.00	$157.00	$15.00	$172.00	($ 22.00)
35	$175.00	$157.00	$17.50	$174.50	$ .50
40	$200.00	$157.00	$20.00	$177.00	$ 23.00
45	$225.00	$157.00	$22.50	$179.50	$ 45.50
50	$250.00	$157.00	$25.00	$182.00	$ 68.00

By examining the table, determine how many clocks must be sold in order for the class to start making a profit?

The first profit occurs when **35** clocks are sold.

PROBLEM #2

Once your class members examine this break-even point analysis, they realize that even if all the clocks are sold, they will only make $68.00 profit. Class members decide that they need to earn more profit. They do some comparison shopping in some local retail stores and find similar clocks are priced from $9 to $13. After some discussion, the class decides that the retail price of the clocks should be $10 rather than $5. The price of the product kit, construction costs, and commission percentage remain the same as in the previous problem. Complete the blanks on the chart that follows. Determine what profit/ loss occurs at each of the following sales levels: 5, 10, 15, 20, 30, 40, 50. The profit/loss calculation has already been made when only one clock is sold.

Number of Clocks Sold	Total Revenue at That Sale Volume	Fixed Expenses	Variable Expenses	Total Expenses	Profit/ Loss
1	$ 10.00	$157.00	$ 1.00	$158.00	($148.00)
5	$ 50.00	$157.00	$ 5.00	$162.00	($112.00)
10	$100.00	$157.00	$10.00	$167.00	($ 67.00)
15	$150.00	$157.00	$15.00	$172.00	($ 22.00)
20	$200.00	$157.00	$20.00	$177.00	$ 23.00
30	$300.00	$157.00	$30.00	$187.00	$113.00
40	$400.00	$157.00	$40.00	$197.00	$203.00
50	$500.00	$157.00	$50.00	$207.00	$293.00

By examining the table, determine how many clocks must be sold in order for the class to start making a profit. (Hint: You may have to do some additional calculations to determine the exact number of clocks that must be sold before your class starts to make a profit.)

The first profit occurs when **18** clocks are sold.

From the table, students should realize that a profit occurs between 16 and 20 clock sales. If they start with 16 sales and continue making calculations until a profit occurs, they would have the following results:

Number of Clocks Sold	Total Revenue at That Sale Volume	Fixed Expenses	Variable Expenses	Total Expenses	Profit/ Loss
16	$160.00	$157.00	$16.00	$173.00	($ 13.00)
17	$170.00	$157.00	$17.00	$174.00	($ 4.00)
18	$180.00	$157.00	$18.00	$175.00	$ 5.00

INSTRUCTIONS

Based on problems #1 and #2, answer the following questions

1. Why can't an entrepreneur ordinarily reach the break-even point by selling just a few items?

   Entrepreneurs cannot recoup both fixed and variable costs by selling just a few product.

2. Why did the group in problem #2 reach the break-even point before the group in problem #1?

   The group in problem #2 recouped their variable and fixed costs sooner because they charged more for the product than the group in problem #1 ($10.00 rather than $5.00). The variable costs were higher per unit, but the revenue generated per unit was also higher for the group in problem #2.

Calculating Break-Even Points

INSTRUCTIONS

Use the following formula to calculate the break-even point:

BREAK-EVEN POINT =

$$\frac{\text{FIXED EXPENSES}}{1 - (\text{VARIABLE EXPENSES} / \text{SALES REVENUE})}$$

1. An entrepreneur has calculated fixed expenses for his planned business at $5,500. Variable expenses have been estimated at $7,900. If total sales revenue is estimated at $18,000, what is the break-even point? (Round-off your calculations to three decimal places.)

    _____

    _____

    _____

2. A business is selling only one product that has a retail price of $10. Fixed expenses for the business are $50,600. Variable expenses have been estimated at $30,400. If sales are planned at $100,000, how many products must be sold before the firm starts earning a profit?

    _____

    _____

3. Your class is selling clocks. Your group plans to sell 50 clocks for $5 each. Fixed expenses are $157, and variable expenses are $25. How many clocks will your class members have to sell before they start earning a profit?

    _____

    _____

    _____

4. Your class is selling clocks. Your group plans to sell 50 clocks for $20 each. Fixed expenses are $157, and variable expenses are $50. How many clocks will your class members have to sell before they start earning a profit?

    _____

    _____

    _____

Calculating Break-Even Points (Answer Key)

INSTRUCTIONS

Use the following formula to calculate the break-even point:

BREAK-EVEN POINT =

$$\frac{\text{FIXED EXPENSES}}{1 - (\text{VARIABLE EXPENSES} / \text{SALES REVENUE})}$$

1. An entrepreneur has calculated fixed expenses for his planned business at $5,500. Variable expenses have been estimated at $7,900. If total sales revenue is estimated at $18,000, what is the break-even point? (Round-off your calculations to three decimal places.)

    $9,804

2. A business is selling only one product that has a retail price of $10. Fixed expenses for the business are $50,600. Variable expenses have been estimated at $30,400. If sales are planned at $100,000, how many products must be sold before the firm starts earning a profit?

    7,271 (Round-off the answer since a fraction of a product cannot be sold)

3. Your class is selling clocks. Your group plans to sell 50 clocks for $5 each. Fixed expenses are $157, and variable expenses are $25. How many clocks will your class members have to sell before they start earning a profit?

    35 (Round-off the answer since a fraction of a product cannot be sold)

4. Your class is selling clocks. Your group plans to sell 50 clocks for $20 each. Fixed expenses are $157, and variable expenses are $50. How many clocks will your class members have to sell before they start earning a profit?

    9 (Round-off the answer since a fraction of a product cannot be sold)

LESSON PLAN V
ACCOUNTING

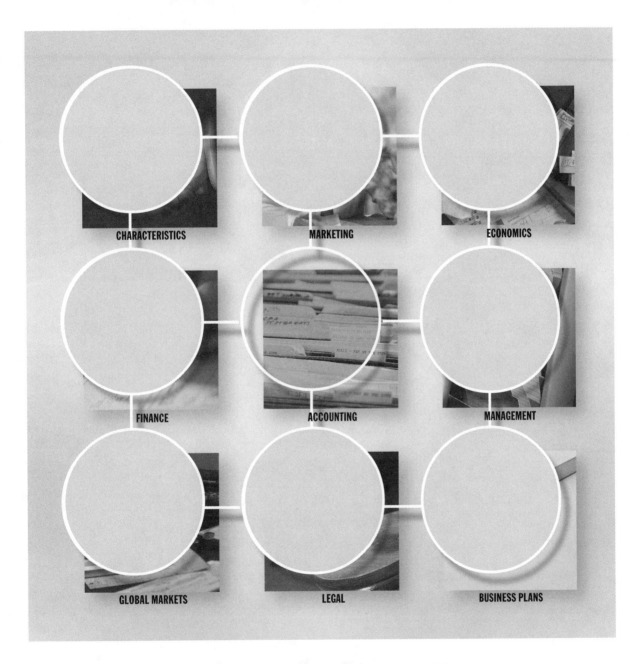

CHARACTERISTICS

MARKETING

ECONOMICS

FINANCE

ACCOUNTING

MANAGEMENT

GLOBAL MARKETS

LEGAL

BUSINESS PLANS

HANDOUTS

Expert Cleaning Service
Income Statement

Expert Cleaning Service
Income Statement
For Month Ended October 31

<u>Revenue</u>

Sales		$9,500.00

<u>Operating Expenses</u>

Supplies	$ 500.00	
Payroll	$1,500.00	
Advertising	$ 250.00	
Insurance	$ 125.00	
Accounting and Legal	$ 75.00	
Miscellaneous	$ 250.00	
Total Expenses		$2,700.00
Net Income		$6,800.00

Expert Cleaning Service
Income Statement

Expert Cleaning Service
Income Statement
For Month Ended November 30

<u>Revenue</u>

Sales	$8,500.00

<u>Operating Expenses</u>

Supplies	$ 600.00	
Payroll	$2,000.00	
Advertising	$ 275.00	
Insurance	$ 125.00	
Accounting and Legal	$ 75.00	
Miscellaneous	$ 500.00	
Total Expenses		$3,575.00
Net Income		$4,925.00

Expert Cleaning Service
Cash Flow Statement

Expert Cleaning Service
Cash Flow Statement
For Month Ended October 31

Sources of Cash

Sales	$5,500.00	
Additional Investment	$1,000.00	
		$6,500.00

Disbursements

Supplies	$ 500.00	
Payroll	$1,500.00	
Advertising	$ 250.00	
Insurance	$ 125.00	
Accounting and Legal	$ 75.00	
Miscellaneous	$ 250.00	
Total Cash Disbursements		$2,700.00
Net Increase in Cash		$3,800.00

Expert Cleaning Service Projected Cash Flow Statement (Answer Key)

Expert Cleaning Service
Projected Cash Flow Statement
For Month Ended November 30

Sources of Cash

Sales ($9,500 x 60%)		$5,700.00

Disbursements

Supplies	$1,000.00	
Payroll	$1,500.00	
Advertising	$ 500.00	
Insurance	$ 125.00	
Accounting and Legal	$ 75.00	
Miscellaneous	$ 250.00	
Payment to Creditors	$1,000.00	
Total Cash Disbursements		$4,450.00
Estimated Increase in Cash		$1,250.00

Expert Cleaning Service
Balance Sheet

Expert Cleaning Service
Balance Sheet
October 31

Assets

Cash	$15,100.00	
Accounts Receivable	$ 4,000.00	
Supplies	$ 1,500.00	
Van	$16,000.00	
Cleaning Equipment	$ 4,000.00	
Total Assets		$40,600.00

Liabilities

Accounts Payable – Jones Supply Co.	$ 4,600.00	
Accounts Payable – King Auto Sales	$11,000.00	
Total Liabilities		$15,600.00

Owners' Equity

John Smith, Capital	$18,200.00	
Net Income	$ 6,800.00	
Total Owner's Equity		$25,000.00
Total Liabilities and Equity		$40,600.00

Expert Cleaning Service Income Statement, Cash Flow Statement, and Balance Sheet

Expert Cleaning Service
Income Statement
For Month Ended October 31

Revenue

Sales	$9,500.00

Operating Expenses

Supplies	$ 500.00
Payroll	$1,500.00
Advertising	$ 250.00
Insurance	$ 125.00
Accounting and Legal	$ 75.00
Miscellaneous	$ 250.00
Total Expenses	$2,700.00
Net Income	$6,800.00

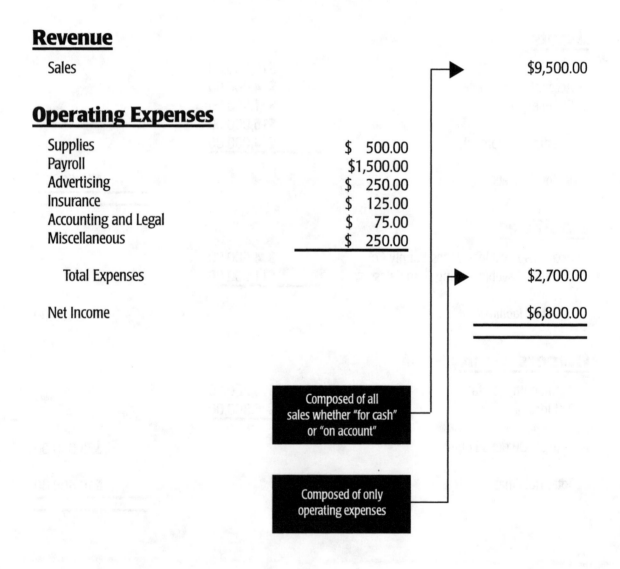

Composed of all sales whether "for cash" or "on account"

Composed of only operating expenses

Income Statement will show profit from operations whether received or not.

Expert Cleaning Service
Cash Flow Statement
For Month Ended October 31

Sources of Cash

Sales	$5,500.00	
Additional Investment	$1,000.00	
Total Sources of Cash		$6,500.00

Disbursements

Supplies	$ 500.00	
Payroll	$1,500.00	
Advertising	$ 250.00	
Insurance	$ 125.00	
Accounting and Legal	$ 75.00	
Miscellaneous	$ 250.00	
Payment to Creditors	$ 1,000.00	
Cash Disbursements		$3,700.00
Net Increase in Cash		$2,800.00

Composed of only "cash" received

Composed of all cash going out

Cash Flow Statement will show actual cash coming in and cash going out.

Expert Cleaning Service
Balance Sheet
October 31

Assets

Cash	$15,100.00	
Accounts Receivable	$ 4,000.00	
Supplies	$ 1,500.00	
Van	$16,000.00	
Cleaning Equipment	$ 4,000.00	
Total Assets		$40,600.00

Liabilities

Accounts Payable — Jones Supply Co.	$ 4,600.00	
Accounts Payable — King Auto Sales	$11,000.00	
Total Liabilities		$15,600.00

Owners' Equity

John Smith, Capital	$18,200.00	
Net Income	$ 6,800.00	
Total Owners' Equity		$25,000.00
Total Liabilities and Equity		$40,600.00

Net Income will ultimately increase the equity in the business.

Practice Problems

Instructions

Using the information provided, calculate the following:

1. The records of Easy Day Care Center show revenue for the month of June at $5,500. Operating Expenses for the same period were $3,300. Was there a net profit or net loss for the period and in what amount?

_____

2. Easy Day Care Center reported revenue and expenses for the following months: July — (r) 6,075.00 (e) 4,008.00; August — (r) 3,086.00 (e) 3,690.00; September — (r) 5,550.00 (e) 5,330.00. Which month during the quarter was the most profitable?

_____

3. Jamie recently opened his service to care for plants after school and on Saturdays. He has always dreamed of owning his own business and now the opportunity is at hand. His business has been in operation for three months, and he is anxious to see if he has made any profit. His records show he has sales in the amount of $890.00. His records show he spent $125.00 on pots for replanting; $35.00 for fertilizer; $85.00 for miscellaneous; and $75.00 on gas for his truck. Did Jamie make any money during his first quarter of operation? If so, how much profit did he realize? If not, how much did he lose?

_____

4. Referring to the above information, Jamie discovered at the end of the quarter that the majority of his revenue was "on account," meaning that it had been charged. As a matter of fact, $650.00 of the $890.00 sales were on account. He quickly realized he needed to look at his cash flow. Did Jamie have a positive or a negative cash flow for the period?

_____

5. If Company A has a total of $75,000 in assets and a total of $28,000 in liabilities, what is the Owner's Equity at the present time?

_____

6. Judy needed to earn money to help with her college expenses. During her senior year of high school and the summer months before leaving home, she decided to open a delivery service for local businesses. Judy's business operated after school for five days a week and then all day during the summer. Judy had often heard her father wish he had some way to get mail to the post office or to have supplies picked up. Deciding there was a market, Judy began by advertising in the local paper and on the radio. Soon her business was well underway. By the time she was ready to leave home, the business reported the following assets: Cash, $2,000.00; Delivery Pickup, $7,500.00; Accounts Receivable, $480.00; Supplies, $70.00. She still owed $3,000.00 on her truck and had one last payment of $25.00 to the Office Supply Company. From the above information, what was Judy's business worth?

_____

Practice Problems (Answer Key)

Instructions

Using the information provided, calculate the following:

1. The records of Easy Day Care Center show revenue for the month of June at $5,500. Operating Expenses for the same period were $3,300. Was there a net profit or net loss for the period and in what amount?

   The was a net profit of $2,200 for the month of June.

2. Easy Day Care Center reported revenue and expenses for the following months: July — (r) 6,075.00   (e) 4,008.00; August — (r) 3,086.00 (e) 3,690.00; September — (r) 5,550.00 (e) 5,330.00. Which month during the quarter was the most profitable?

   July was the most profitable month.
   July net profit $2,067
   August net loss .... ($604)
   September net profit $220

3. Jamie recently opened his service to care for plants after school and on Saturdays. He has always dreamed of owning his own business and now the opportunity is at hand. His business has been in operation for three months, and he is anxious to see if he has made any profit. His records show he has sales in the amount of $890.00. His records show he spent $125.00 on pots for replanting; $35.00 for fertilizer; $85.00 for miscellaneous; and $75.00 on gas for his truck. Did Jamie make any money during his first quarter of operation? If so, how much profit did he realize? If not, how much did he lose?

   Yes, Jamie realized a profit of $570.

4. Referring to the above information, Jamie discovered at the end of the quarter that the majority of his revenue was "on account," meaning that it had been charged. As a matter of fact, $650.00 of the $890.00 was on account. He quickly realized he needed to look at his cash flow. Did Jamie have a positive or a negative cash flow for the period?

   Negative cash flow (cash from current sales $890 - $650 = $240 minus expense of $320 means a negative cash flow.)

5. If Company A has a total of $75,000 in assets and a total of $28,000 in liabilities, what is the Owner's Equity at the present time?

   $75,000 - $28,000 = $47,000

6. Judy needed to earn money to help with her college expenses. During her senior year of high school and the summer months before leaving home, she decided to open a delivery service for local businesses. Judy's business operated after school for five days a week and then all day during the summer. Judy had often heard her father wish he had some way to get mail to the post office or to have supplies picked up. Deciding there was a market, Judy began by advertising in the local paper and on the radio. Soon her business was well underway. By the time she was ready to leave home, the business reported the following assets: Cash, $2,000.00; Delivery Pickup, $7,500.00; Accounts Receivable, $480.00; Supplies, $70.00. She still owed $3,000.00 on her truck and had one last payment of $25.00 to the Office Supply Company. From the above information, what was Judy's business worth?

   $10,050 (assets) - $3,025 (liabilities) = $7,025

The Scratch Pad — A Case Study

To meet the growing demand for personalized notepaper, greeting cards, invitations and other items, Cynthia and Davis Barkley open a small printing business called The Scratch Pad in their community. Residents had often remarked that it was inconvenient to drive into the city to buy small items for gifts and special occasions. With the advanced technology available to the Barkleys, their dream of opening their own business became reality three years ago.

To date, the Barkleys employ only one person and own a small building on Main Street. Business is fairly stable throughout the year with holidays generating more business. The news of their business has traveled to surrounding communities, which has resulted in an increase in the number of customers.

At present, the Barkleys are ready to close their books for the last quarter. It is your responsibility to prepare the financial statements for the quarter. Using the following information, prepare an income statement and cash flow statement for this quarter.

Sales for the quarter end were $32,000. The Scratch Pad offers sales on account to special customers. For this quarter, the records are showing the amount of charged sales to be $28,000. They figure that $24,000 was paid during the quarter on sales made in previous quarters. The operating expenses for the quarter were: Supplies, $5,300; Wages, $3,400; Utilities, $1,450; Insurance, $300; Advertising, $500; Equipment Maintenance, $1,700; Miscellaneous, $350. These were all paid in cash during the quarter. The Barkleys also made a payment of $3,000 on the loan they secured from Enterprise Bank to purchase their building. Another check was written to the Computer Store in the amount of $550 to reduce the debt on their equipment.

Once you have prepared the income statement and the cash flow statement for the period, the Barkleys are anxious for you to prepare an updated balance sheet. Records provide the following information: Cash, $9,000; Accounts Receivable, $30,000; Supplies, $3,500; Equipment, $5,500; Building, $60,000; and Liabilities of Enterprise Bank, $24,000; Computer Store, $1,900.

The Scratch Pad Income Statement (Answer Key)

**The Scratch Pad
Income Statement
For Quarter Ended December 31**

Revenue

Sales	$32,000.00

Operating Expenses

Supplies	$5,300.00
Wages	$3,400.00
Utilities	$1,450.00
Insurance	$ 300.00
Advertising	$ 500.00
Equipment Maintenance	$1,700.00
Miscellaneous	$ 350.00
Total Expense	$13,000.00
Net Income	$19,000.00

The Scratch Pad Cash Flow Statement (Answer Key)

The Scratch Pad
Cash Flow Statement
For Quarter Ended December 31

Sources of Cash

Sales $28,000.00

Disbursements

Supplies	$5,300.00	
Wages	$3,400.00	
Utilities	$1,450.00	
Insurance	$ 300.00	
Advertising	$ 500.00	
Equipment Maintenance	$1,700.00	
Miscellaneous	$ 350.00	
Payment on Loan	$3,000.00	
Accounts Payable	$ 550.00	
Cash Disbursements		$16,550.00
Net Increase in Cash		$11,450.00

The Scratch Pad Balance Sheet (Answer Key)

The Scratch Pad
Balance Sheet
December 31

Assets

Cash	$ 9,000.00	
Accounts Receivable	$30,000.00	
Supplies	$ 3,500.00	
Equipment	$ 5,500.00	
Building	$60,000.00	
Total Assets		$108,000.00

Liabilities

Accounts Payable — Enterprise Bank	$24,000.00	
Accounts Payable — Computer Store	$ 1,900.00	
Total Liabilities		$ 25,900.00

Owners' Equity

Total Owners' Equity		$ 82,100.00
Total Liabilities and Owners' Equity		$108,000.00

Calculating Sales Trends

Sales cannot be forecast with absolute accuracy; yet, business owners must make educated guesses. One helpful guide is the average rate of increase or decrease in sales from one period of time to another. In the chart below are a firm's sales figures for each quarter last year. Sales figures are also listed for the first three quarters of this year.

	Sales Last Year	Sales This Year
1st Quarter	$50,000	$62,000
2nd Quarter	$55,000	$63,000
3rd Quarter	$59,000	$64,000
4th Quarter	$60,000	????????

INSTRUCTIONS

Calculate the percentage of sales increase or decrease from one quarter to the next. That percentage is calculated using the following formula:

% of Sales Increase or Decrease = Difference in sales for two periods / Sales for first period

EXAMPLE

Calculate the sales increase/decrease in the sales from the 1st quarter to the 2nd quarter of last year.

Your calculation would be as follows:
($55,000 - $50,000) / $50,000 = 10% increase

ANSWER THE FOLLOWING QUESTIONS

1. Calculate the percentage of sales increase/ decrease for the 2nd quarter (last year) to the 3rd quarter (last year).

_____

2. Calculate the percentage of sales increase/ decrease for the 3rd quarter (last year) to the 4th quarter (last year).

_____

3. Calculate the percentage of sales increase/ decrease for the 4th quarter (last year) to the 1st quarter (this year).

_____

4. Calculate the percentage of sales increase/ decrease for the 1st quarter (this year) to the 2nd quarter (this year).

_____

5. Calculate the percentage of sales increase/ decrease for the 2nd quarter (this year) to the 3rd quarter (this year).

_____

6. Calculate the percentage of sales increase/ decrease for the 1st quarter (last year) to the 1st quarter (this year).

_____

7. Calculate the percentage of sales increase/ decrease for the 2nd quarter (last year) to the 2nd quarter (this year).

_____

8. Calculate the percentage of sales increase/ decrease for the 3rd quarter (last year) to the 3rd quarter (this year).

_____

9. What would you forecast (predict) that sales would be for the 4th quarter (this year)? Explain your rationale.

_____

_____

_____

_____

10. In making this sales forecast, what other factors would you want to consider before making your prediction?

_____

_____

_____

_____

11. If sales in the 3rd quarter (this year) had been $60,000, how would the forecast for the 4th quarter be affected?

_____

_____

_____

_____

Calculating Sales Trends (Answer Key)

Sales cannot be forecast with absolute accuracy; yet, business owners must make educated guesses. One helpful guide is the average rate of increase or decrease in sales from one period of time to another. In the chart below are a firm's sales figures for each quarter last year. Sales figures are also listed for the first three quarters of this year.

	Sales Last Year	Sales This Year
1st Quarter	$50,000	$62,000
2nd Quarter	$55,000	$63,000
3rd Quarter	$59,000	$64,000
4th Quarter	$60,000	????????

INSTRUCTIONS

Calculate the percentage of sales increase or decrease from one quarter to the next. That percentage is calculated using the following formula:

% of Sales Increase or Decrease = Difference in sales for two periods / Sales for first period

EXAMPLE

Calculate the sales increase/decrease in the sales from the 1st quarter to the 2nd quarter of last year.

Your calculation would be as follows:
($55,000 - $50,000) / $50,000 = 10% increase

ANSWER THE FOLLOWING QUESTIONS

1. Calculate the percentage of sales increase/ decrease for the 2nd quarter (last year) to the 3rd quarter (last year).

   ($59,000 -$55,000) / $55,000 = 7.3% increase

2. Calculate the percentage of sales increase/ decrease for the 3rd quarter (last year) to the 4th quarter (last year).

   ($60,000 - $59,000) / $59,000 = 1.7% increase

3. Calculate the percentage of sales increase/ decrease for the 4th quarter (last year) to the 1st quarter (this year).

   ($62,000 - $60,000) / $60,000 = 3.3% increase

4. Calculate the percentage of sales increase/ decrease for the 1st quarter (this year) to the 2nd quarter (this year).

   ($63,000 - $62,000) / $62,000 = 1.6% increase

5. Calculate the percentage of sales increase/ decrease for the 2nd quarter (this year) to the 3rd quarter (this year).

   ($64,000 - $63,000) / $63,000 = 1.6% increase

6. Calculate the percentage of sales increase/ decrease for the 1st quarter (last year) to the 1st quarter (this year).

   ($62,000 - $50,000) / $50,000 = 24.0% increase

7. Calculate the percentage of sales increase/ decrease for the 2nd quarter (last year) to the 2nd quarter (this year).

   ($63,000 - $55,000) / $55,000 = 14.5% increase

8. Calculate the percentage of sales increase/ decrease for the 3rd quarter (last year) to the 3rd quarter (this year).

($64,000 - $59,000) / $59,000 = 8.5% increase

9. What would you forecast (predict) that sales would be for the 4th quarter (this year)? Explain your rationale.

Answers will vary. When sales last year are compared with sales this year, they have slowed considerably from the 1st quarter. At the beginning of the year, sales had increased 24% over last year; however, by the 3rd quarter, sales had only increased by 8.5%. Also, in the two most recent periods (1st quarter to 2nd quarter and 2nd quarter to 3rd quarter), sales have only increased by 1.6% each period. (Students should realize that forecasting does not involve random guessing. Analyzing past sales data usually provides a range in which their prediction will fall. For this situation, their prediction should be between 1.6% and 8.5%, but probably closer to 1.6%.)

10. In making this sales forecast, what other factors would you want to consider before making your prediction?

Business owners also want to consider any changes in what the business is doing that would affect sales such as more advertising, longer hours, new product introductions, etc. They would also want to consider any changes in economic and market conditions that would affect sales such as new competition entering the market, recessions, increased prosperity in an area, heavy advertising by the competition, etc.

11. If sales in the 3rd quarter (this year) had been $60,000, how would the forecast for the 4th quarter be affected?

The most recent sales data indicate a decline in sales; however, a trend cannot be predicted based on only one quarter. Those figures may simply be an anomaly. But the data would probably cause the owner to estimate no sales increase for the fourth quarter.

Conditions That Affect Sales Forecasts

Instructions

Identify all the conditions and events that would affect sales at the school's concession stand at football games during the season. List each answer under the internal or external factors category.

Internal Factors	External Factors

Forecasting Sales

DIRECTIONS

In the spaces below, record the actual daily sales figures (provided by your instructor) for one item being sold in your school cafeteria or concession stand.

Item: _____

Actual Daily Sales (Units) Last Week:

Monday _____

Tuesday _____

Wednesday _____

Thursday _____

Friday _____

INSTRUCTIONS

In the first column of the chart below, record your individual sales forecast (in units) for this week of this same item. In a team of four (4), make the same forecasts. Record your team predictions in Column 2. All the members of your team must agree on each forecast. DO NOT CHANGE ANY INDIVIDUAL FORECASTS YOU MADE IN THE FIRST COLUMN. Give this handout to your instructor. Next week, you will complete columns three, four, and five when you will be provided with actual sales figures for this week.

	Column 1 Individual Forecast	Column 2 Group Forecast	Column 3 Actual Forecast	Column 4 Difference Between Individual Forecast and Actual Sales	Column 5 Difference Between Group Forecast and Actual Sales
Monday					
Tuesday					
Wednesday					
Thursday					
Friday					
Totals					

Tracking Inventory

INSTRUCTIONS

Using the following information, complete the inventory record below.

Beginning inventory for January was 5 units.

Monthly purchases in units were:
January	20
February	20
March	30
April	35
May	35
June	45

Demand in units was:
January	18
February	19
March	35
April	35
May	39
June	43

INVENTORY RECORD

	January	February	March	April	May	June
Beginning Inventory						
Purchases						
Available for Sale						
Sales						
Ending Inventory						

Tracking Inventory (Answer Key)

INSTRUCTIONS

Using the following information, complete the inventory record below.

Beginning inventory for January was 5 units.

Monthly purchases in units were:
January	20
February	20
March	30
April	35
May	35
June	45

Demand in units was:
January	18
February	19
March	35
April	35
May	39
June	43

INVENTORY RECORD

	January	February	March	April	May	June
Beginning Inventory	5	7	8	3	3	0
Purchases	20	20	30	35	35	45
Available for Sale	25	27	38	38	38	45
Sales	18	19	35	35	38	43
Ending Inventory	7	8	3	3	0	2

At What Price Will I Make a Profit?

PROBLEM #1

Complete the following monthly profit/loss statements based on the following information. Each item cost $40. Monthly expenses associated with the item were $845 each for January and February, and $1,000 each for March through June.

Monthly unit sales at an $80 retail price were:

January 18
February 19
March 35
April 35
May 38
June 43

MONTHLY PROFIT/LOSS STATEMENTS

	January	February	March	April	May	June
Sales ($)						
Cost of Goods Sold						
Gross Margin						
Expenses						
Profit/Loss						

PROBLEM #2

Complete the following monthly profit/loss statements based on the following information. Each item cost $40. Monthly expenses associated with the item were $845 each for January and February, and $1,000 each for March through June.

Monthly unit sales at an $60 retail price were:

January	23
February	23
March	39
April	39
May	46
June	49

MONTHLY PROFIT/LOSS STATEMENTS

	January	February	March	April	May	June
Sales ($)						
Cost of Goods Sold						
Gross Margin						
Expenses						
Profit/Loss						

At What Price Will I Make a Profit? (Answer Key)

PROBLEM #1

Complete the following monthly profit/loss statements based on the following information. Each item cost $40. Monthly expenses associated with the item were $845 each for January and February, and $1,000 each for March through June.

Monthly unit sales at an $80 retail price were:

January 18
February 19
March 35
April 35
May 38
June 43

MONTHLY PROFIT/LOSS STATEMENTS

	January	February	March	April	May	June
Sales ($)	$1,440	$1,520	$2,800	$2,800	$3,040	$3,440
Cost of Goods Sold	$ 720	$ 760	$1,400	$1,400	$1,520	$1,720
Gross Margin	$ 720	$ 760	$1,400	$1,400	$1,520	$1,720
Expenses	$ 845	$ 845	$1,000	$1,000	$1,000	$1,000
Profit/Loss	($ 125)	($ 85)	$ 400	$ 400	$ 520	$ 720

PROBLEM #2

Complete the following monthly profit/loss statements based on the following information. Each item cost $40. Monthly expenses associated with the item were $845 each for January and February, and $1,000 each for March through June.

Monthly unit sales at an $60 retail price were:
January 23
February 23
March 39
April 39
May 46
June 49

MONTHLY PROFIT/LOSS STATEMENTS

	January	February	March	April	May	June
Sales ($)	$1,380	$1,380	$2,340	$2,340	$2,760	$2,940
Cost of Goods Sold	$ 920	$ 920	$1,560	$1,560	$1,840	$1,960
Gross Margin	$ 460	$ 460	$ 780	$ 780	$ 920	$ 980
Expenses	$ 845	$ 845	$1,000	$1,000	$1,000	$1,000
Profit/Loss	($ 385)	($ 385)	($ 220)	($ 220)	($ 80)	($ 20)

Putting It All Together — Profitable Forecasting and Purchasing

You have the responsibility for buying and pricing skateboards in the sporting goods department at the department store in your town. You must develop a purchasing plan based on past sales records, as well as the most recent sales trends. Last year's monthly sales records for skateboards are listed below. Last year, skateboards had a retail price of $60 the entire year. Throughout the year, skateboards will cost you $45. This is the same cost your firm paid last year.

Month	Unit Sales
January	14
February	21
March	23
April	25
May	29
June	30
July	30
August	32
September	32
October	34
November	38
December	43

In this simulation, your decisions will involve buying and pricing merchandise. In addition, you must update inventory forms and complete monthly profit/loss statements to determine if your decisions are profitable. You will begin the simulation on January 1. You do not have any skateboards in stock to begin the year. At the beginning of each month, you must make the following decisions:

1. Forecast (estimate) sales for the month.

2. Subtract beginning inventory from your sales forecast. This figure represents the number of skateboards to be ordered. Record this number under units ordered on Form A, which follows.

3. Next, determine the retail price for the skateboards. Your retail price must be one of the following:
   $45 $50 $55 $60 $65 $70 $75
   Record this number under retail price on Form A.

4. Your instructor will then provide you with the demand figures at the retail price that you have established. Write this number on a separate sheet of paper. This is NOT sales unless you have enough inventory in stock.

5. Now, update your inventory record (Form B), with purchases for the month and sales based on the demand figure you received from your instructor. Remember that you can only sell what you have in stock. If demand is higher than your inventory, you have missed potential sales.

6. At this point, all that you know is how much you sold. Sales do NOT equal profits. Business owners must use accounting forms to determine if their decisions yield a profit. Complete the monthly profit/loss statement found on Form C.

7. At this point, you are ready to make your purchasing and pricing decisions for the next month. You may need to change your retail price in order to earn a profit. Continue this process until you have completed the year.

FORM A — MAKING PURCHASING DECISIONS AND ESTABLISHING RETAIL SALES

	January	February	March	April	May	June	July	August	September	October	November	December
Units Ordered												
Retail Price												

FORM B — INVENTORY RECORD

	January	February	March	April	May	June	July	August	September	October	November	December
Beginning Inventory												
Purchases												
Available for Sale												
Sales												
Ending Inventory												

FORM C – MONTHLY PROFIT/LOSS STATEMENT

	January	February	March	April	May	June	July	August	September	October	November	December
Sales												
Cost of Good Sold												
Gross Margin												
Expenses	$350	$350	$350	$350	$350	$350	$350	$350	$350	$350	$350	$350
Profit/Loss												

LESSON PLAN VI
MANAGEMENT

CHARACTERISTICS

MARKETING

ECONOMICS

FINANCE

ACCOUNTING

MANAGEMENT

GLOBAL MARKETS

LEGAL

BUSINESS PLANS

HANDOUTS

Should an Employee Be Added?

INSTRUCTIONS

Read the following cases and indicate whether an employee should be added. Be sure to indicate the reasons for your responses.

1. Juan has a well-known antique store in an urban area. He runs the shop by himself and has done a good job of building up the business throughout the years. Individuals from all over the area come to his shop to buy collectible items. They like dealing with him. However, Juan is finding that the hours are becoming very long. His shop is open seven hours a day (10 a.m. to 5 p.m.) for five days during the week. Also, many weeks he spends two to three nights meeting with individuals or going to auctions in order to buy items for the shop. He is thinking about hiring someone for 14 hours a week (two days). His net income from the shop is $25,000 a year. He would be paying this new employee about $120 a week in wages and fringe benefits. Would you recommend that Juan hire a new employee? Why or why not?

_____

_____

_____

_____

_____

2. Melody opened a restaurant featuring foods from other countries. She has found that there is an increasing amount of business. Currently, the restaurant is open from 10 a.m. to 4 p.m. — serving breakfast and lunch daily. She only employs one other person who is the cook. She wants to hire another food preparer/cook. A problem she is encountering is slow service; food is not prepared quickly enough. A considerable number of people walk out of her restaurant because of this delay. She would like the individual to work eight hours a day and thinks it will cost her $320 per week, which would include the employee's pay plus fringe benefits. Currently, her income from the business is $40,000. She thinks that an additional $20,000 in revenues will be generated by adding a competent employee. Would you recommend that Melody hire a new employee? Why or why not?

_____

_____

_____

_____

_____

_____

Should an Employee Be Added? (Answer Key)

INSTRUCTIONS

Read the following cases and indicate whether an employee should be added. Be sure to indicate the reasons for your responses.

1. Juan has a well-known antique store in an urban area. He runs the shop by himself and has done a good job of building up the business throughout the years. Individuals from all over the area come to his shop to buy collectible items. They like dealing with him. However, Juan is finding that the hours are becoming very long. His shop is open seven hours a day (10 a.m. to 5 p.m.) for five days during the week. Also, many weeks he spends two to three nights meeting with individuals or going to auctions in order to buy items for the shop. He is thinking about hiring someone for 14 hours a week (two days). His net income from the shop is $25,000 a year. He would be paying this new employee about $120 a week in wages and fringe benefits. Would you recommend that Juan hire a new employee? Why or why not?

Answers will vary. On the one hand, Juan could hire a new employee so as to give him more free time. He would be giving up $6,240 in income but it might be worth it. Revenues, at least in the short run, would probably not increase because his customers are accustomed to talking with Juan, not a clerk. Eventually, there might be more customers and increased revenue if the new employee is trusted and valued by customers. On the other hand, $6,240 is a lot of money. In order to have more time to enjoy life, Juan should determine when he is not very busy and make it a policy to close the store at those times. For example, on Monday through Thursday, he might have fewer customers in the morning. Juan might decide to open the shop at 12:00 noon instead of 10:00 a.m. on these days. He may lose some revenue because of lost sales but it would probably be minimal.

2. Melody opened a restaurant featuring foods from other countries. She has found that there is an increasing amount of business. Currently, the restaurant is open from 10 a.m. to 4 p.m. — serving breakfast and lunch daily. She only employs one other person who is the cook. She wants to hire another food preparer/cook. A problem she is encountering is slow service; food is not prepared quickly enough. A considerable number of people walk out of her restaurant because of this delay. She would like the individual to work eight hours a day and thinks it will cost her $320 per week, which would include the employee's pay plus fringe benefits. Currently, her income from the business is $40,000. She thinks that an additional $20,000 in revenues will be generated by adding a competent employee. Would you recommend that Melody hire a new employee? Why or why not?

Answers will vary. On the one hand, Melody could hire an additional employee since she is losing customers, which is damaging the reputation of her business. On the other hand, hiring a new employee could be a poor financial decision. Melody will pay $16,640 in wages and fringe benefits for the new employee yet she estimates to generate only $20,000 in revenues. Also, after factoring in the additional costs for food service, there is very little net profit. However, it could be argued that the minimal additional profit is necessary to restore the restaurant's reputation. In time, Melody may want to raise prices to improve the profit picture. Customers would probably pay slightly higher prices for the specialized food served at the restaurant.

Job Responsibilities and Skills

INSTRUCTIONS

Read each case problem and answer the questions.

1. Mary has been running a pet shop by herself for several years. She is getting tired of the long hours and would like to have someone else run the store for 20 hours during the week and longer hours during peak times, such as around the December holidays. She wants this person to do many of the tasks that she does during the day which include opening and closing the store, waiting on customers, cleaning cases, identifying when animals are sick, administering medicines to animals when necessary, keeping records, and keeping the store clean.

List this person's duties, as well as the skills, understandings, and attitudes that he or she will need for the job.

Responsibilities	Skills

2. Aaron designs Web pages for businesses in the area. He works out of his home and has been surprised at how many clients he has. In fact, he is having trouble doing both the contact work with customers or possible clients and the development of the Web pages on the computer. He would like to hire someone to work for him in his home developing Web pages while he is calling on individuals. The prospective employee should have a good understanding of computers, visual design, people, telephone communications, and the Internet. What are the responsibilities and skills necessary to succeed in this position?

Responsibilities	Skills

Job Responsibilities and Skills (Answer Key)

INSTRUCTIONS

Read each case problem and answer the questions.

1. Mary has been running a pet shop by herself for several years. She is getting tired of the long hours and would like to have someone else run the store for 20 hours during the week and longer hours during peak times, such as around the December holidays. She wants this person to do many of the tasks that she does during the day which include opening and closing the store, waiting on customers, cleaning cases, identifying when animals are sick, administering medicines to animals when necessary, keeping records, and keeping the store clean.

List this person's duties, as well as the skills, understandings, and attitudes that he or she will need for the job.

Responsibilities	Skills
Opening and closing store	Proven track record of being dependable
Waiting on customers	Enjoys working with people and gets along well with others
Cleaning cages	Does not mind distasteful task and genuinely loves animals
Identifying when animals are sick	Has experience working with animals and sufficient familiarity with them to identify when they are ill
Administering medicine to animals	Has patience and interest to give animals medicine they might not want but need
Keeping records	Has patience in keeping clerical records and is honest
Keeping store clean	Displays a willingness to do janitorial work and has a sense of cleanliness that is consistent with the owner's views

2. Aaron designs Web pages for businesses in the area. He works out of his home and has been surprised at how many clients he has. In fact, he is having trouble doing both the contact work with customers or possible clients and the development of the Web pages on the computer. He would like to hire someone to work for him in his home developing Web pages while he is calling on individuals. The prospective employee should have a good understanding of computers, visual design, people, telephone communications, and the Internet. What are the responsibilities and skills necessary to succeed in this position?

Responsibilities	Skills
Good understanding of computer	Is able to work with hardware and software packages
Work with visual design	Knows visual design principles that are attractive for Web pages
Work with people	Pleasant manner with people, understands what they want, and is patient with customer requests
Use phone effectively	Good phone etiquette — knows when to limit conversation and how to use phone effectively
Use Internet successfully	Knows how to put information on and take information off the Internet

What Do Your Friends, Family, and Teachers Think About Work?

INSTRUCTIONS

Set up interviews with three people to discuss their reasons for working.

PERSON #1

Age Group —
  16 – 18   18 – 22
  22 – 30   Over 30

1.

   _____

   _____

2.

   _____

   _____

3.

   _____

   _____

PERSON #2

Age Group —
  16 – 18   18 – 22
  22 – 30   Over 30

1.

   _____

   _____

2.

   _____

   _____

3.

   _____

   _____

PERSON #3

Age Group —
  16 – 18   18 – 22
  22 – 30   Over 30

1.

   _____

   _____

2.

   _____

   _____

3.

   _____

   _____

Extrinsic and Intrinsic Rewards

Responsibilities	Extrinsic	Intrinsic
Employee of the month		
Sense of achievement		
Corner office		
Promotion		
Pride		
Raise in pay		
Recognition at monthly sales meeting		
Doing a job well		
Trip to Hawaii for winning sales contest		
Letter of congratulation from company CEO		
Feeling of belonging to the team		
Reaching your potential		

Extrinsic and Intrinsic Rewards (Answer Key)

Responsibilities	Extrinsic	Intrinsic
Employee of the month	✓	
Sense of achievement		✓
Corner office	✓	
Promotion	✓	
Pride		✓
Raise in pay	✓	
Recognition at monthly sales meeting	✓	
Doing a job well		✓
Trip to Hawaii for winning sales contest	✓	
Letter of congratulation from company CEO	✓	
Feeling of belonging to the team		✓
Reaching your potential		✓

Managerial Strategies – Theory X or Y?

Strategy	Theory X	Theory Y
Employees sign in and out		
Employees receive weekly updates		
Employees must ask permission to use company files		
Employees are given performance goals for the month		
Creativity is encouraged		
Employees are given both bad and good news		
Supervisor is always right		
Employees set their own goals and standards of performance		
Doctors' excuses are required for absences		
Work goals are set by supervisors		

Managerial Strategies — Theory X or Y? (Answer Key)

Strategy	Theory X	Theory Y
Employees sign in and out	✓	
Employees receive weekly updates		✓
Employees must ask permission to use company files	✓	
Employees are given performance goals for the month	✓	
Creativity is encouraged		✓
Employees are given both bad and good news		✓
Supervisor is always right	✓	
Employees set their own goals and standards of performance		✓
Doctors' excuses are required for absences	✓	
Work goals are set by supervisors	✓	

Vision Statements

ST. LOUIS PARK TOMORROW VISION

"Vision St. Louis Park" is a community-wide strategic planning effort aimed at ensuring a bright future for St. Louis Park. In August 1996, a vision statement was adopted by the members of "Vision St. Louis Park," a group of individuals representing government, schools, businesses, community organizations, religious institutions, and St. Louis Park residents.

In early 1995, task forces began formulating specific recommendations to move our community from its vision of the future to reality. In all, hundreds of suggestions were drafted. Today, the city, schools, businesses, and community organizations are working to implement these suggestions.

Our Vision for the Future St. Louis Park — Our Community of Choice for a Lifetime. . .

. . .Diversity is a natural part of everyday life that enriches the entire community. Community leaders are as diverse as St. Louis Park's population. Community decisions are made within a caring framework of mutual understanding and respect.

. . .Responsive service is a hallmark of city government. City government provides valued service by continuously assessing the community's current needs and anticipating future needs. City government is enriched by citizen participation, positive community leadership, and active collaborations and partnerships.

. . .Our community is a safe environment in which to live, work, and learn. Safety is the result of an active partnership among citizens, businesses, community organizations, and law enforcement agencies working together to solve problems and prevent crime.

. . .Educational opportunities for all ages abound because a high value is placed on education. Quality lifelong learning results from collaboration among schools — both public and private — families, neighborhoods, businesses, city government, and community institutions.

. . .Children are a top priority for the entire community. Families, schools, city government, community institutions, and businesses are actively involved in creating an environment that enables children to build the assets they need to succeed.

. . .A wide spectrum of quality housing is available to meet residents' housing needs through all stages of life. City government, businesses, and local institutions work together to ensure there is a range of financial and structure choices in housing.

. . .Business provides a solid base for the community and benefits from strong support from residents, schools, and government. Residents' retail and service needs are met within the community. Businesses, community organizations, schools, and city government work together to create household supporting jobs, spur desirable business growth, and address environmental challenges.

. . .Residents have strong connections to the community thanks to community pride, civic commitment, mutual respect, and neighborliness. Individuals, neighborhoods, and community institutions work to enhance the community, solve problems, and address environmental challenges.

MICROSOFT CORPORATION VISION

At Microsoft Corporation our long-held vision of a computer on every desk and in every home continues to be at the core of everything we do. We are committed to the belief that software is the tool that empowers people both at work and at home. Since our company was founded in 1975, our charter has been to deliver this vision of the power of personal computing.

As the world's leading software provider, we strive to continually produce innovative products that meet the evolving needs of our customers. Our extensive commitment to research and development is coupled with dedicated responsiveness to customer feedback. This allows us to explore future technological advancements, while assuring that our customers today receive the highest quality software produces.

TACOM-ARDEC VISION

The vision of TACOM-ARDEC is to be. . .
. . .Recognized internationally as the world leader for technology, design, development, engineering and production, and field support in assigned armament systems;

. . .Recognized by our Nation and customers as a center of technical excellence, providing work of exceptional quality, an outstanding return on investment, and "Making a Difference" in the battlefield superiority of U.S. Armed Forces;

. . .Recognized for aggressively ensuring that all resources are properly managed;

. . .Valued by our employees for providing challenging and rewarding opportunities in a safe and supportive work environment; and

. . .Acknowledged as maintaining the highest standards of integrity, honesty, and trust.

EDUTECH VISION

EduTech will be one of the top five places in the world that develops and implements innovative and effective applications of technology to education. Its special emphasis will be on applying what we know about how people learn to the development of effective learning environments. The influence of these cognitive principles will be seen in the development of curricula; innovative pedagogical principles and practices; and software, multimedia, and networking tools. EduTech will concentrate on the education of Georgia Tech students, taking seriously also the dissemination of its results to local elementary and secondary schools, industrial training programs, and other postsecondary colleges and universities. EduTech's efforts will include both research into relevant educational issues and implementation of new educational programs and technology.

What Are the Most Important Goals?

INSTRUCTIONS

Read the vision statements listed below and indicate which of the following goals would probably be most important for each organization. A goal may be important to more than one organization. Be prepared to provide reason(s) for your responses. For marking your paper, use the following key:

A — St. Louis Park Tomorrow
B — Microsoft Corporation
C — Tacom-Ardec
D — EduTech
E — All of the above

1. Develop quality software

_____

2. Develop community spirit

_____

3. Provide quality education

_____

4. Know the latest in educational theory

_____

5. Provide quality service

_____

6. Provide a safe environment

_____

7. Know changes that are taking place in the Armed Forces of our country

_____

8. Knowledge of current technology

_____

9. Celebration of diversity within the organization

_____

10. New teaching practices

_____

What Are the Most Important Goals? (Answer Key)

INSTRUCTIONS

Read the vision statements listed below and indicate which of the following goals would probably be most important for each organization. A goal may be important to more than one organization. Be prepared to provide reason(s) for your responses. For marking your paper, use the following key:

A — St. Louis Park Tomorrow
B — Microsoft Corporation
C — Tacom-Ardec
D — EduTech
E — All of the above

1. Develop quality software

    B — Microsoft Corporation and D — EduTech

2. Develop community spirit

    A — St. Louis Park Tomorrow

3. Provide quality education

    A — St. Louis Park Tomorrow and D — EduTech

4. Know the latest in educational theory

    D — EduTech

5. Provide quality service

    E — All of the above

6. Provide a safe environment

    A — St. Louis Park Tomorrow and C — Tacom-Ardec

7. Know changes that are taking place in the Armed Forces of our country

    C — Tacom-Ardec

8. Knowledge of current technology

    B — Microsoft Corporation, C — Tacom-Ardec, and D — EduTech

9. Celebration of diversity within the organization

    A — St. Louis Park Tomorrow

10. New teaching practices

    A — St. Louis Park Tomorrow and D — EduTech

The Efficient Repairer

INSTRUCTIONS

Read the Vision Statement and answer the questions that follow.

The purpose of The Efficient Repairer is to provide quality, efficient, and economical repair of electric typewriters and calculators. The firm provides this service through well-educated repair people who know the products because of training provided by the manufacturers of the machinery, extensive experience in the field, and a well-stocked library of repair manuals for many different brands of typewriters and calculators.

We maintain quality tools and equipment to fix typewriters and calculators. This means repairs can be made by our firm in less time than by our competitors. Our concern for safety has paid off in that the no customers or employees of the firm have ever had any serious accidents.

1. What are the goals of this business?

_____

_____

_____

_____

_____

2. Do you think the firm should continue to have this vision statement? Why or why not?

_____

_____

_____

_____

_____

The Efficient Repairer (Answer Key)

INSTRUCTIONS

Read the Vision Statement and answer the questions that follow.

The purpose of The Efficient Repairer is to provide quality, efficient, and economical repair of electric typewriters and calculators. The firm provides this service through well-educated repair people who know the products because of training provided by the manufacturers of the machinery, extensive experience in the field, and a well-stocked library of repair manuals for many different brands of typewriters and calculators.

We maintain quality tools and equipment to fix typewriters and calculators. This means repairs can be made by our firm in less time than by our competitors. Our concern for safety has paid off in that the no customers or employees of the firm have ever had any serious accidents.

1. What are the goals of this business?

   Possible Answers: Provide quality, quick service at the lowest price for the repair of typewriters and calculators. Train their service technicians to be experts in this field.

2. Do you think the firm should continue to have this vision statement? Why or why not?

   Eventually, the firm will have to change its vision statement since the demand for typewriters and calculators is decreasing as personal computers become more affordable and accessible.

LESSON PLAN VII
GLOBAL MARKETS

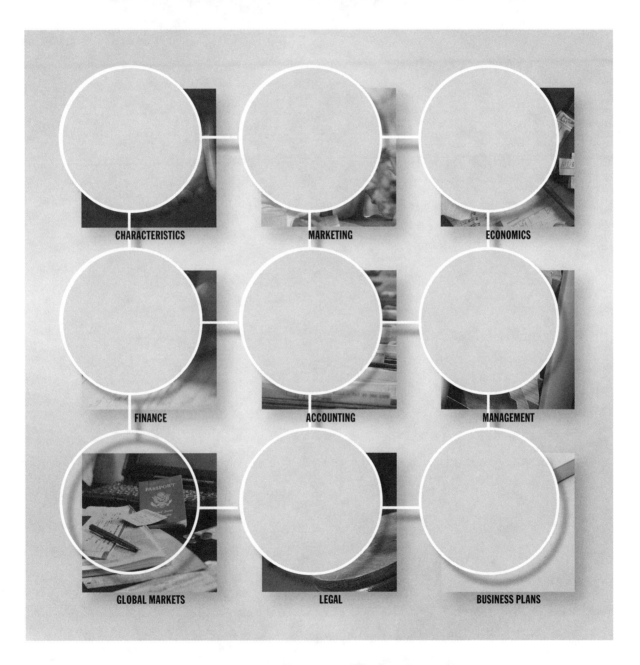

CHARACTERISTICS

MARKETING

ECONOMICS

FINANCE

ACCOUNTING

MANAGEMENT

GLOBAL MARKETS

LEGAL

BUSINESS PLANS

HANDOUTS

Big U.S. Players in the Global Game

INSTRUCTIONS

Analyze the table below and answer the following questions.

Company	Foreign Revenues (Percent of Total)	Foreign Profits (Percent of Total)	Foreign Assets (Percent of Total)
E.I. du Pont de Nemours	51.4%	99.6%	37.3%
Procter & Gamble	52.1%	65.1%	40.7%
Coca-Cola	67.0%	67.8%	48.6%
Eastman Kodak	48.8%	41.5%	32.4%
Motorola	43.9%	84.8%	34.6%
Johnson & Johnson	49.1%	54.6%	43.9%
Sara Lee	35.5%	41.3%	45.0%
Colgate-Palmolive	64.5%	67.0%	46.9%
Gillette	67.5%	61.4%	65.7%
Compaq Computer	49.0%	63.6%	40.5%
McDonald's	46.9%	45.1%	46.9%
Avon Products	32.0%	59.9%	48.3%

1. Which firms earn more than half of their revenues from foreign sales?

_____

_____

2. Which firms earn more than half of their profits from foreign sales?

_____

_____

Source: Adapted from the 100 Largest Multinationals: Getting the Welcome Carpet. *Forbes.* July 18, 1994. 276-79.

Big U.S. Players in the Global Game (Answer Key)

INSTRUCTIONS

Analyze the table below and answer the following questions.

Company	Foreign Revenues (Percent of Total)	Foreign Profits (Percent of Total)	Foreign Assets (Percent of Total)
E.I. du Pont de Nemours	51.4%	99.6%	37.3%
Procter & Gamble	52.1%	65.1%	40.7%
Coca-Cola	67.0%	67.8%	48.6%
Eastman Kodak	48.8%	41.5%	32.4%
Motorola	43.9%	84.8%	34.6%
Johnson & Johnson	49.1%	54.6%	43.9%
Sara Lee	35.5%	41.3%	45.0%
Colgate-Palmolive	64.5%	67.0%	46.9%
Gillette	67.5%	61.4%	65.7%
Compaq Computer	49.0%	63.6%	40.5%
McDonald's	46.9%	45.1%	46.9%
Avon Products	32.0%	59.9%	48.3%

1. Which firms earn more than half of their revenues from foreign sales?

   E.I. du Pont de Nemours, Procter & Gamble, Coca-Cola, Colgate Palmolive, and Gillette

2. Which firms earn more than half of their profits from foreign sales?

   All of them except Eastman Kodak, Sara Lee, and McDonald's

Source: Adapted from the 100 Largest Multinationals: Getting the Welcome Carpet. *Forbes*. July 18, 1994. 276-79.

The Globalization of the American Economy

INSTRUCTIONS

Read the article below and answer the following questions.

America's involvement in the global economy has passed through two distinct periods: a development era during which the U.S. sought industrial self-sufficiency in the 18th and 19th centuries, and a free-trade era in the early and middle 20th century during which open trade was linked with prosperity. Now America has entered a third, more dangerous era — an age of global economic interdependence.

With surprising swiftness, the U.S. has shifted from relative economic self-sufficiency to global interdependence. In 1960, trade accounted for only 10 percent of the country's gross national product; by the mid-1980s, that figure had more than doubled. American farmers now sell 30 percent of their grain production overseas; 40 percent of U.S. farmland is devoted to crops for export. In fact, more acres of U.S. farmland are used to feed the Japanese than there are acres of farmland in Japan. American industry exports more than 20 percent of its manufacturing output, and the Department of Commerce estimates that, on average, 19,100 jobs result for every $1 billion of merchandise exports. More than 70 percent of American industry now faces stiff foreign competition within the U.S. market.

1. The author indicates that the U.S. has entered a more dangerous era — an age of global economic interdependence. Why is it more dangerous?

_____

_____

_____

_____

_____

2. What is an indicator that American industry is becoming more internationalized?

_____

_____

_____

_____

_____

Sources: Adapted from Pat Choate and Juyne Linger. Tailored Trade: Dealing With the World as It Is. *Harvard Business Review*, January – February 1988. 87-88; and U.S. Trade Facts. *Business America*, April 6, 1992. 34.

The Globalization of the American Economy (Answer Key)

INSTRUCTIONS

Read the article below and answer the following questions.

America's involvement in the global economy has passed through two distinct periods: a development era during which the U.S. sought industrial self-sufficiency in the 18th and 19th centuries, and a free-trade era in the early and middle 20th century during which open trade was linked with prosperity. Now America has entered a third, more dangerous era — an age of global economic interdependence.

With surprising swiftness, the U.S. has shifted from relative economic self-sufficiency to global interdependence. In 1960, international trade accounted for only 10 percent of the country's gross national product; by the mid-1980s, that figure had more than doubled. American farmers now sell 30 percent of their grain production overseas; 40 percent of U.S. farmland is devoted to crops for export. In fact, more acres of U.S. farmland are used to feed the Japanese than there are acres of farmland in Japan. American industry exports more than 20 percent of its manufacturing output, and the Department of Commerce estimates that, on average, 19,100 jobs result for every $1 billion of merchandise exports. More than 70 percent of American industry now faces stiff foreign competition within the U.S. market.

1. The author indicates that the U.S. has entered a more dangerous era — an age of global economic interdependence. Why is it more dangerous?

   More competition and interdependence. With competition there is the possibility that one cannot do as well as others. With interdependence, another nation on which you depend for goods/services may turn out to be undependable.

2. What is an indicator that American industry is becoming more internationalized?

   In the mid-1980s, trade accounted for 20 percent of the Gross National Product (GNP), whereas in the 1960s it was 10 percent — there has been tremendous increases in the amounts of agriculture and manufacturing items sold in other countries.

Sources: Adapted from Pat Choate and Juyne Linger. Tailored Trade: Dealing With the World as It Is. *Harvard Business Review*, January – February 1988. 87-88; and U.S. Trade Facts. *Business America*, April 6, 1992. 34.

Green — A Double Whammy

INSTRUCTIONS

Read the article below and answer the following questions.

The trend in many U.S. communities is to visit a foreign county in a search for foreign trade. These trips can prove that sometimes the simplest thing can cause problems. For example, a county commissioner and 20 business representatives seeking business connections arrived in Taiwan bearing gifts of green baseball caps.

The trip was scheduled a month before elections. No one knew that green was the color of the political opposition party. In addition, the visitors learned too late that, according to Taiwan culture, a man wears green to signify that his wife has been unfaithful. "I don't know whatever happened to those green hats but the trip gave us an understanding of the extreme differences in our culture," said the county commissioner. While a green hat may spell trouble in Taiwan, the color green symbolizes exuberance and youth in other Asian countries.

1. What should have been done before bringing gifts into that country?

_____

_____

_____

_____

_____

_____

2. Is giving gifts acceptable as a business practice in the U.S.?

_____

_____

_____

_____

_____

_____

Source: From a public address and Roger Axtell. *The Do's and Taboos of International Trade.* John Wiley and Sons. New York, 1994. 227.

Green — A Double Whammy (Answer Key)

INSTRUCTIONS

Read the article below and answer the following questions.

The trend in many U.S. communities is to visit a foreign county in a search for foreign trade. These trips can prove that sometimes the simplest thing can cause problems. For example, a county commissioner and 20 business representatives seeking business connections arrived in Taiwan bearing gifts of green baseball caps.

The trip was scheduled a month before elections. No one knew that green was the color of the political opposition party. In addition, the visitors learned too late that, according to Taiwan culture, a man wears green to signify that his wife has been unfaithful. "I don't know whatever happened to those green hats but the trip gave us an understanding of the extreme differences in our culture," said the county commissioner. While a green hat may spell trouble in Taiwan, the color green symbolizes exuberance and youth in other Asian countries.

1. What should have been done before bringing gifts into that country?

   Research the proper protocol for giving gifts in that country.

2. Is giving gifts acceptable as a business practice in the U.S.?

   Yes, gift giving is done in the U.S. Recently, however, legislation was passed that placed restrictions on the dollar amount of the gift.

Source: From a public address and Roger Axtell. *The Do's and Taboos of International Trade*. John Wiley and Sons. New York, 1994. 227.

Factors Associated With the Culture of a Country

Culture is the society's program for survival, the accepted basis for responding to external and internal events.

FACTORS

Geography and Climate

_____

_____

Business Protocol

_____

_____

Political Structure

_____

_____

Economic Base

_____

_____

Legal System

_____

_____

History

_____

_____

Resources

_____

_____

Social Responsibility

_____

_____

Economic Growth

_____

_____

Environmental Management

_____

_____

Language

_____

_____

Tradition and Customs

_____

_____

Religious Beliefs

_____

_____

Embracing Cultural Diversity

INSTRUCTIONS

Read the following paragraph and answer the questions.

Value judgements should not be made based on ethnic or cultural differences. People around the world feel as strongly about their cultures as we do about ours. Every country thinks its culture is the best and for every foreign peculiarity that amuses us, there is an American peculiarity that amuses others. The Chinese tell American dog jokes, reflecting their amazement that we could feel the way we do about an animal that the Chinese consider better for eating than petting. And we're surprised that the French take their dogs to the finest restaurants, where the dogs might be served at the table.

1. What are some American cultural behaviors or events that other countries might not understand?

   _____

   _____

   _____

   _____

   _____

2. What are some cultural activities in other countries that Americans might not understand?

   _____

   _____

   _____

   _____

   _____

Sources: Adapted from Lennie Copeland and Lewis Griggs. *Going International*. Random House. New York. 1985. 43.

Embracing Cultural Diversity (Answer Key)

INSTRUCTIONS

Read the following paragraph and answer the questions.

Value judgements should not be made based on ethnic or cultural differences. People around the world feel as strongly about their cultures as we do about ours. Every country thinks its culture is the best and for every foreign peculiarity that amuses us, there is an American peculiarity that amuses others. The Chinese tell American dog jokes, reflecting their amazement that we could feel the way we do about an animal that the Chinese consider better for eating than petting. And we're surprised that the French take their dogs to the finest restaurants, where the dogs might be served at the table.

1. What are some American cultural behaviors or events that other countries might not understand?

   Cleanliness of Americans; some American food, such as pizza and hamburger — cows are considered sacred in some cultures.

2. What are some cultural activities in other countries that Americans might not understand?

   Reverence for royalty and cows.

Sources: Adapted from Lennie Copeland and Lewis Griggs. *Going International.* Random House. New York. 1985. 43.

Is a Cheeto a Cheeto if It Doesn't Taste Like Cheese?

INSTRUCTIONS

Read the article below and answer the following questions.

PepsiCo, the creator of Cheetos, announces a $1 million joint venture to produce a little cripsy-tasting cheese puff in the Guangdong province of China. The estimated market for Western snack foods in the Guangdong province is $40 to $70 million. The province, with 70 million consumers, represents a market that is one-third the size of the U.S. Between-meal snacking is rising rapidly, along with disposable income as the Chinese economy gains momentum and work hours increase.

This is the first time a major snack-food brand will be produced in China for Chinese tastes. In adapting Cheetos to the Chinese market, a new flavor had to be found. Cheese is not a mainstay in the Chinese diet and, in focus groups, the cheese-ish taste of American Cheetos did not test well. More than 600 flavors, ranging from Roasted Cuttlefish to Sweet Caramel were tested before settling on Savory American Cream (a buttered popcorn flavor) and Zesty Japanese Steak (a teriyaki-type taste)

But is it a Cheeto if it doesn't taste like cheese? "It's still crispy, it has a Cheeto shape, and it's fun to eat, so it's a Cheeto," says the general manager of PepsiCo Foods International.

The introduction of Cheetos will be backed by television, print advertising, and promotions based on Chester Cheetah, the brand's feline symbol, riding a Harley-Davidson motorcycle. The packages will carry the Cheeto logo in English, along with the Chinese characters qi duo, which translate to new surprise.

Source: Adapted from Glenn Collins. Chinese to Get a Taste of Cheese-Less Cheetos. *The New York Times*. September 2, 1994. C4.

1. Why was Pepsi interested in the Chinese market for their Cheetos?

_____

_____

_____

_____

_____

2. What extra efforts did Pepsi undertake in order to sell Cheetos in the Chinese market?

_____

_____

_____

_____

3. What would you have done before proceeding with the advertising of the new Cheetos in China?

_____

_____

_____

_____

Is a Cheeto a Cheeto if It Doesn't Taste Like Cheese? (Answer Key)

INSTRUCTIONS

Read the article below and answer the following questions.

PepsiCo, the creator of Cheetos, announces a $1 million joint venture to produce a little cripsy-tasting cheese puff in the Guangdong province of China. The estimated market for Western snack foods in the Guangdong province is $40 to $70 million. The province, with 70 million consumers, represents a market that is one-third the size of the U.S. Between-meal snacking is rising rapidly, along with disposable income as the Chinese economy gains momentum and work hours increase.

This is the first time a major snack-food brand will be produced in China for Chinese tastes. In adapting Cheetos to the Chinese market, a new flavor had to be found. Cheese is not a mainstay in the Chinese diet and, in focus groups, the cheese-ish taste of American Cheetos did not test well. More than 600 flavors, ranging from Roasted Cuttlefish to Sweet Caramel were tested before settling on Savory American Cream (a buttered popcorn flavor) and Zesty Japanese Steak (a teriyaki-type taste)

But is it a Cheeto if it doesn't taste like cheese? "It's still crispy, it has a Cheeto shape, and it's fun to eat, so it's a Cheeto," says the general manager of PepsiCo Foods International.

The introduction of Cheetos will be backed by television, print advertising, and promotions based on Chester Cheetah, the brand's feline symbol, riding a Harley-Davidson motorcycle. The packages will carry the Cheeto logo in English, along with the Chinese characters qi duo, which translate to new surprise.

1. Why was Pepsi interested in the Chinese market for their Cheetos?

   Pepsi was interested in the Chinese market for the following reasons: market size; the lack of competition in the snack food area; and the Chinese were interested in purchasing snack foods due to the increase in disposable income and between-meal eating.

2. What extra efforts did Pepsi undertake in order to sell Cheetos in the Chinese market?

   Pepsi spent considerable time testing different flavors for the Chinese market. They also developed a new advertising program for this market.

3. What would you have done before proceeding with the advertising of the new Cheetos in China?

   Possible answers include complete research on the use of TV and print advertising. Research the acceptance of using Chester Cheetah for the advertising. Complete test marketing on the sample advertisement.

Source: Adapted from Glenn Collins. Chinese to Get a Taste of Cheese-Less Cheetos. *The New York Times*. September 2, 1994. C4.

Coke's Back and Still Has the Secret

INSTRUCTIONS

Read the article below and answer the following questions.

For 91 years, the formula for Coca-Cola has been a closely guarded secret. Then the government of India ordered Coca-Cola to disclose it or cease operations in that country. A secret ingredient, cal 7-X, supposedly gives Coke its distinctive flavor. The government's minister for industry told the Indian parliament that Coca-Cola's Indian branch would have to transfer 60 percent of its equity shares to Indians and hand over its know-how by April 1978, or shut down. Indian sales accounted for less than one percent of Coca-Cola's worldwide sales. The potential market in India, a country of 800 million, is tremendous.

The government refused to let the branch import the necessary ingredients, and Coke — once as abundant as bottled drinking water sold in almost every Indian town of more than 50,000 — packed up their bags and left the country. The minister for industry said the Coca-Cola activities in India "… furnish a classic example of how multinational corporations operating in a low-priority, high-profit area in a developing country attain run-away growth and … trifle with the weaker indigenous industry." Coke said they wouldn't give up the formula and India said they had to leave.

Sixteen years later, India's attitude toward foreign investment changed and Coke reentered the market without having to divulge its formula. During Coke's 16-year exile, however, Pepsi Cola came to India and captured a 26 percent market share. Not to worry, there is plenty of market for both considering India's per capita consumption is just three eight-ounce bottles a year, versus about 12 for Pakistan and 731 in the U.S.

1. What cultural factor(s) in India affected Coca-Cola?

_____

_____

_____

_____

_____

2. Why do you think India made all these demands of Coca-Cola?

_____

_____

_____

_____

_____

3. Do you think Coca-Cola should have given the Indian government their secret ingredient?

_____

_____

_____

_____

_____

Sources: Indian Government Rejects Coke's Bid to Sell Soft Drinks. *The Wall Street Journal*, March 16, 1990, p. B5; and Coke Adds Fizz to India. *Fortune*, January 10, 1997, pp. 14-15.

Coke's Back and Still Has the Secret (Answer Key)

INSTRUCTIONS

Read the article below and answer the following questions.

For 91 years, the formula for Coca-Cola has been a closely guarded secret. Then the government of India ordered Coca-Cola to disclose it or cease operations in that country. A secret ingredient, cal 7-X, supposedly gives Coke its distinctive flavor. The government's minister for industry told the Indian parliament that Coca-Cola's Indian branch would have to transfer 60 percent of its equity shares to Indians and hand over its know-how by April 1978, or shut down. Indian sales accounted for less than one percent of Coca-Cola's worldwide sales. The potential market in India, a country of 800 million, is tremendous.

The government refused to let the branch import the necessary ingredients, and Coke — once as abundant as bottled drinking water sold in almost every Indian town of more than 50,000 — packed up their bags and left the country. The minister for industry said the Coca-Cola activities in India "… furnish a classic example of how multinational corporations operating in a low-priority, high-profit area in a developing country attain run-away growth and … trifle with the weaker indigenous industry." Coke said they wouldn't give up the formula and India said they had to leave.

Sixteen years later, India's attitude toward foreign investment changed and Coke reentered the market without having to divulge its formula. During Coke's 16-year exile, however, Pepsi Cola came to India and captured a 26 percent market share. Not to worry, there is plenty of market for both considering India's per capita consumption is just three eight-ounce bottles a year, versus about 12 for Pakistan and 731 in the U.S.

1. What cultural factor(s) in India affected Coca-Cola?

   India's political and legal systems.

2. Why do you think India made all these demands of Coca-Cola?

   The demands were probably made because Coca-Cola was making so much money which was decreasing the sales of domestically-produced drinks. In other words, Coca-Cola overpowered their Indian competitors in the marketplace.

3. Do you think Coca-Cola should have given the Indian government their secret ingredient?

   Answers will vary. By not revealing their ingredient, Coca-Cola left the market, giving up their market share which may be difficult to recapture. On the other hand, their product might have been easily replicated if they revealed the secret ingredient.

Sources: Indian Government Rejects Coke's Bid to Sell Soft Drinks. *The Wall Street Journal*, March 16, 1990, p. B5; and Coke Adds Fizz to India. *Fortune*, January 10, 1997, pp. 14-15.

Project Guidelines for Assessing a Foreign Market

INSTRUCTIONS

1. This project maybe done individually or in groups of three to five students.

2. Select a product (good/service) that you want to market in another country. It can be a product already in existence or one that is new. If you have difficulty selecting an item, your teacher will give you some suggestions.

3. Determine one country where the product is not now marketed but probably could be quite popular. Write down reasons why you want to start selling the product in this country.

4. Determine information about the culture of that country from various sources. Use the cultural factors already discussed in class as the framework in which to gain your information. For example, gain information about government, economic systems, traditions, etc. This information can be researched from a variety of sources. For example:

    a. Interview local individual businesses doing business with that country to describe the various cultural factors of that country.

    b. Conduct an Internet search for information on that country. One Internet address to use for gaining such information is: http//www.stat-usa.gov/.

    c. Ask your librarian for sources. The *Statistical Abstract of the U.S. Culture Grams* and *PC Globe* are some possibilities.

5. Determine what you must do differently with the product/service in order for it to be successfully accepted in that foreign country. To demonstrate this, you might want to develop some sample advertising, jingles, or recommend new types of packaging for the product. Or you might suggest some changes to the product itself.

6. Each team will make a presentation to the class on the conclusions of their research. It can be done in the form of a team report with an optional PowerPoint presentation or a role-playing situation. Each team should make sure that the following areas are covered in the presentation:

    Selected product.
    Selected target country.
    Conclusions of research regarding facts about the country's culture.
    Modifications made in the production or marketing of the product in order to ensure success for sales in that foreign country.
    Prediction of success for the entrepreneur.

To Trade or Not to Trade

INSTRUCTIONS

Imagine that there are only two islands in the world. Breadburg is where the Breadburgers live, and Fishmong is inhabited by the Fishmongers. The names of the villages show the type of goods that they are best able to produce. The Breadburgers have rich soil, not very rocky, which is excellent for raising small grains which they use to make breads. Their fishing is also good. The Fishmongers, though, live on an island which is almost all rocks. Their primary source for supporting themselves is fishing.

Each island has about 100 people. It has been determined how much fish or bread each island economy could produce each day.

Breadburgers — 500 loaves of bread or 200 pounds of fish.

Fishmongers — 40 loaves of bread or 100 pounds of fish.

At the present time, the islands do not trade with one another. In your group, please make the following decisions:

1. The two countries could decide to start trading with one another. If they start trading, assume that one loaf of bread equals one pound of fish. Do you think they should start trading or not? Explain reasons for your decisions.

2. Based on your decision in #1 — for an entire week, what do you think they should produce — fish or bread or a combination thereof? Provide the production you would recommend for each island for a given week considering five days to be the workweek.

Review Questions

1. What is the difference between imports and exports?

   _____

   _____

   _____

   _____

2. Explain the concept of economic interdependence of nations.

   _____

   _____

   _____

3. Define comparative advantage, and list three products in the production of which the U.S. has such an advantage.

   _____

   _____

   _____

   _____

4. Name one advantage consumers derive from international trade and one that nations derive.

   _____

   _____

   _____

   _____

   _____

5. What disadvantages, if any, does trade have for producers, workers, and nations?

   _____

   _____

   _____

   _____

   _____

Trade Concerns of the Breadburgers and the Fishmongers

The Fishmongers and the Breadburgers decided a few years ago that life would be much better for both of them if they started to trade. So they did. The population of both islands began enjoying a higher standard of living than ever before. But some concerns arose that needed attention. Read each of the questions below and develop answers.

1. The Fishmongers found that they were running out of items to pay their government workers. They want to raise additional taxes by charging for each loaf of bread that is sold from the Breadburgers. They would like to charge the Breadburgers one quarter of a loaf as taxes for each loaf of bread they sell in Fishmong. That quarter loaf would then be given to the government workers as additional pay. Should they do this or not? Why?

   _____

   _____

   _____

   _____

   _____

2. The citizens of Breadburg who were fisherpeople are disgusted. With increased trade between the islands, it was better for Breadburg to start producing only bread and trading it for fish from the Fishmongers. The former fisherpeople of Breadburg were forced to become farmers and bakers, which they did not like. They are now lobbying the government to let only so many fish from the Fishmongers be sold to Breadburg residents. They argue that it is important that the fishing industry be started up again on Breadburg island, especially if problems arise between the two islands. They reason that if the two islands get into war, the Fishmongers may discontinue selling fish to Breadburg. Fish is a very important source of protein in the diet of the Breadburg residents. They would indeed suffer from a lack of protein, at least for awhile, if the Fishmongers did not produce fish, relying primarily on the Fishmongers for their fish supply. Thus, they would like to see the fishing industry come back. Do you believe they should institute this policy? Explain.

   _____

   _____

   _____

   _____

   _____

3. Some of the residents of Breadburg are upset because bands from Fishmong are coming over in the late evening to steal bread. They want the government to show their disappointment with Fishmongers by not importing any more of their fish. Do you think this policy should be implemented? Explain.

_____

_____

_____

_____

_____

4. Indicate how the three above illustrations demonstrate ways in which government can affect international trade. Name the three ways and indicate what effect each has on the working of international trade.

_____

_____

_____

_____

_____

5. Develop arguments for and against using various governmental regulations to curb trade between and among nations.

_____

_____

_____

_____

_____

Trade Concerns of the Breadburgers and the Fishmongers (Answer Key)

The Fishmongers and the Breadburgers decided a few years ago that life would be much better for both of them if they started to trade. So they did. The population of both islands began enjoying a higher standard of living than ever before. But some concerns arose that needed attention. Read each of the questions below and develop answers.

1. The Fishmongers found that they were running out of items to pay their government workers. They want to raise additional taxes by charging for each loaf of bread that is sold from the Breadburgers. They would like to charge the Breadburgers one quarter of a loaf as taxes for each loaf of bread they sell in Fishmong. That quarter loaf would then be given to the government workers as additional pay. Should they do this or not? Why?

   Answers will vary according to the opinions of the students. At first glance, it appears that the Fishmongers are getting their increase in the cost of government paid for by the Breadburgers, who are paying the additional tax. Yet, the individuals who actually pay the tax are the consumers in Fishmong, who will be paying higher prices for the bread. That is, the importing firm passes on such taxes to the consumer in higher prices. Consumers generally buy less when the price is high. The Breadburgers will not have to produce as much for the Fishmongers. They will make less profit. Enacting a tax on imports generally promotes a retaliatory effort on the part of the other country. It will, in turn, induce additional taxes on goods/services that are imported into their market. It indeed has an effect of decreasing trade between and among nations.

2. The citizens of Breadburg who were fisherpeople are disgusted. With increased trade between the islands, it was better for Breadburg to start producing only bread and trading it for fish from the Fishmongers. The former fisherpeople of Breadburg were forced to become farmers and bakers, which they did not like. They are now lobbying the government to let only so many fish from the Fishmongers be sold to Breadburg residents. They argue that it is important that the fishing industry be started up again on Breadburg island, especially if problems arise between the two islands. They reason that if the two islands get into war, the Fishmongers may discontinue selling fish to Breadburg. Fish is a very important source of protein in the diet of the Breadburg residents. They would indeed suffer from a lack of protein, at least for awhile, if the Fishmongers did not produce fish, relying primarily on the Fishmongers for their fish supply. Thus, they would like to see the fishing industry come back. Do you believe they should institute this policy? Explain.

   Answers will vary. Governmental regulations, such as quotas, save jobs in specific industries favored by the regulation in the domestic economy. Because of the quota, not enough fish will be imported from Fishmong to meet the wants of Breadburg. Thus, fishing jobs will be created. The cost to Breadburg will be a decrease in the amount of bread which is made because resources will have to be diverted to producing fish. This may be all right with the Breadburgers if they perceive fish as essential for national security. Putting in such quotas, though, is generally retaliatory, meaning that the quotas against one nation encourage that nation to put quotas against imports from other nations. Like the tax situation in the previous example, quotas do restrain trade. Also, such action does not prompt the most efficient use of the nation's resources.

3. Some of the residents of Breadburg are upset because bands from Fishmong are coming over in the late evening to steal bread. They want the government to show their disappointment with Fishmongers by not importing any more of their fish. Do you think this policy should be implemented? Explain.

Answers will vary. Embargoes, implemented by one nation, generally encourage other countries to put in embargoes. If there were two nations and only two goods which were produced between them, the embargo implemented by Breadburg could well generate an embargo by Fishmong against the bread imported from Breadburg. This would, in turn, mean that both countries would have to return to producing both bread and fish for themselves. The standard of living of both nations would then decline.

4. Indicate how the three above illustrations demonstrate ways in which government can affect international trade. Name the three ways and indicate what effect each has on the working of international trade.

Government can affect international trade by (1) tariffs, (2) quotas, and (3) embargoes, which are all shown in the case situation.

5. Develop arguments for and against international trade restrictions.

Arguments for trade restrictions:
Protects industries needed for national security.
Protects infant industries.
Encourages development of a diversified economy.
Encourages a greater variety of jobs.
Protects high wage jobs in the industries protected by the regulation.

Arguments against trade restrictions:
Uses the resources of the nation less efficiently since inefficient industries are protected.
Standard of living is not at optimal level since consumers pay higher prices for certain goods/services due to little competition compared to what the consumer would pay with open trade.
Discourages nations from understanding that they are really very interdependent in this world.

LESSON PLAN VIII
LEGAL

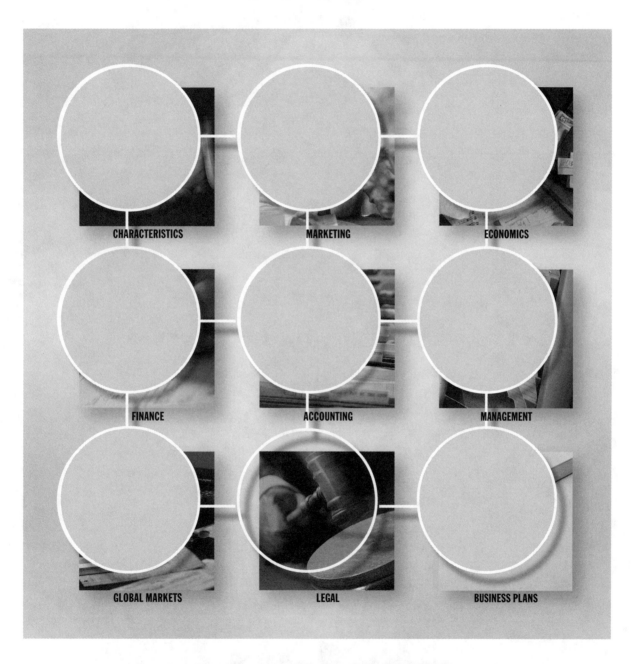

CHARACTERISTICS

MARKETING

ECONOMICS

FINANCE

ACCOUNTING

MANAGEMENT

GLOBAL MARKETS

LEGAL

BUSINESS PLANS

HANDOUTS

Cake Riddles List

1. What would a cake for Gabriel be called?

   _____

2. What would a cake baked by Anita Bryant be called?

   _____

3. What would a cake baked by a geologist be called?

   _____

4. What would a cake baked by a sculptor be called?

   _____

5. What would a cake for little Jack Horner be called?

   _____

6. What would a cake for a monkey be called?

   _____

7. What would a cake for a weight watcher be called?

   _____

8. What would a cake baked for someone who lives off another person's generosity be called?

   _____

9. What would a cake baked for a gossip be called?

   _____

10. What would a cake for the baseball batter who sacrificed himself be called?

    _____

Cake Riddles List (Answer Key)

1. What would a cake for Gabriel be called?

   Angel Food Cake

2. What would a cake baked by Anita Bryant be called?

   Orange Cake

3. What would a cake baked by a geologist be called?

   Layer Cake

4. What would a cake baked by a sculptor be called?

   Marble Cake

5. What would a cake for little Jack Horner be called?

   Plum Cake

6. What would a cake for a monkey be called?

   Banana or Coconut Cake

7. What would a cake for a weight watcher be called?

   Pound Cake

8. What would a cake baked for someone who lives off another person's generosity be called?

   Sponge Cake

9. What would a cake baked for a gossip be called?

   Spice Cake

10. What would a cake for the baseball batter who sacrificed himself be called?

    Bundt Cake

Riddles List

1.

O
―――――――――
Ph.D.
M.A.
B.S.

2.

3.

LE
  VEL

4.

      J
YOU U Me
      S
      T

5.

W
O
R
H
T

6.

T
O
W
N

7.

R
E
T
T
A
B

8.

HE'S HIMSELF

9.

CRAZY
―――――――――
YOU

10.

OATH
―――――――――
UR

Riddles List (Answer Key)

1.

$$\frac{O}{\text{Ph.D. M.A. B.S.}}$$

O
———————
Ph.D.
M.A.
B.S.

2.

3.

LE
  VEL

4.

YOU   J   Me
        U
        S
        T

5.

W
O
R
H
T

6.

T
O
W
N

7.

R
E
T
T
A
B

8.

HE'S HIMSELF

9.

$$\frac{\text{CRAZY}}{\text{YOU}}$$

10.

$$\frac{\text{OATH}}{\text{UR}}$$

Answer Key:
1. Three degrees below zero
2. See-through blouse
3. Split level
4. Just between you and me
5. Throw up
6. Downtown
7. Batter up
8. He's beside himself
9. Crazy over you
10. You are under oath

What Should Anthony Do?

Anthony Graber recently graduated from a local community college with a major in literature. He accepted a permanent position as a reporter with a local paper — the same paper he worked part-time for while going to college.

Recently, Anthony heard that Mr. Savlagito, the owner of the town's pet shop, is interested in retiring in another year. He wants $40,000 for the pet business.

Anthony is excited about the possibility of buying the business from Mr. Savlagito. Anthony worked part-time at the pet shop while attending high school. He loved working there. As a part-time employee, Anthony was responsible for cleaning the animals and their cages.

Anthony estimates Mr. Savlagito makes a modest income of approximately $30,000 to $35,000 per year from his business.

Since Anthony has always wanted to be his own boss, the thought of owning the pet shop is very appealing. He estimates he can save $10,000 this year from his wages at the newspaper since he lives at home with his parents who do not require him to pay rent.

Anthony also thinks his parents will loan him some money and that Mr. Savlagito might be willing to negotiate his selling price. Hal, one of Anthony's friends, has some money saved and might be willing to invest in this business venture. In addition, Hal has experience with running a small business.

If Anthony decides to buy the business, which form of business ownership should he use?

Government's Regulation of Business

INSTRUCTIONS

Your team's task is to research government regulation of business. Answer the following questions:

1. What is the source of the state's power to regulate business?

_____

_____

_____

_____

_____

2. What is the source of the federal government's power to regulate business?

_____

_____

_____

_____

3. Under the Commerce Clause, does the federal government have the power to regulate businesses that conduct all their transactions within the borders of a single state?

_____

_____

_____

_____

_____

4. What reasoning has the U.S. Supreme Court used to justify the extent of the federal government's power to regulate a business that operates only within the borders of a single state?

_____

_____

_____

_____

_____

Patent Protection

INSTRUCTIONS

Your team's task is to research patents. Answer the following questions:

1. What is the definition of a patent?

   _____

   _____

   _____

   _____

   _____

2. What are the requirements of a patent?

   _____

   _____

   _____

   _____

   _____

3. Based upon your understanding of the requirements of a patent, is it possible to patent a living thing? Explain your answer.

   _____

   _____

   _____

   _____

   _____

   _____

4. What are the procedures involved in obtaining a patent?

   _____

   _____

   _____

   _____

   _____

Copyright Protection

Your team's task is to research copyrights. Answer the following questions:

1. What is the definition of a copyright?

   _____

   _____

   _____

   _____

   _____

2. What exclusive legal rights are granted with a copyright?

   _____

   _____

   _____

   _____

   _____

3. Based upon your understanding of the requirements of a copyright, is it possible to copyright computer software? Explain the requirements for copyrighting software.

   _____

   _____

   _____

   _____

   _____

4. What are the procedures involved in obtaining a copyright?

   _____

   _____

   _____

   _____

   _____

Environmental Protection Agency

INSTRUCTIONS

Your team's task is to research the Environmental Protection Agency (EPA). Answer the following questions:

1. What is the definition of an administrative agency?

   _____

   _____

   _____

   _____

2. Where do the administrative agencies get their power?

   _____

   _____

   _____

   _____

3. What is the purpose and function of the EPA?

   _____

   _____

   _____

   _____

   _____

4. What is the extent of power of the EPA?

   _____

   _____

   _____

   _____

5. What federal statute regulates administrative agencies? Explain the extent of that regulation.

   _____

   _____

   _____

   _____

Dialogue – The Dilemma of UBCNA-52094

Dr. Ursula St. James, a microbiologist working for United Biotechnology Corporation of North America (UBCNA), has genetically engineered a new strain of bacteria. Dr. St. James' modification created a type of bacteria that is capable of absorbing air-borne pollutants. As a result, the bacteria can be released into the air to eliminate smog and other pollution in big cities. Naturally, this makes the bacteria, labeled UBCNA-52094, very valuable. Consequently, several different in-house research teams are hard at work attempting to determine the best route to take in marketing the bacteria.

The president of the company has called a meeting of team leaders to discuss the attempt to put UBCNA-52094 on the market. The following people are at the meeting:

- Jane Johnson – UBCNA President
- Ken Hampton – UBCNA Government Regulation Research Team Leader
- Lois Robinson – UBCNA Patent Research Team Leader
- Sam Williams – UBCNA Copyright Research Team Leader
- Kris Styles – UBCNA EPA Research Team Leader

Jane: I'm worried about the government sticking its nose into our attempt to sell UBCNA-52094 to the public. There's a lot of money at stake here, so I want to make sure that we get these bacteria on the market as soon as possible.

Ken: Well, I'm certain that the state will want to regulate the sale of the bacteria. There's no question of its power to regulate us.

Jane: Are you sure about that?

Ken: Well no.

Jane: Then find out. I want to know if the state government has this right.

Ken: Okay, Jane. But what about Washington? Do you want me to look into whether the feds can regulate us, too?

Jane: Definitely. Find out if the feds have the power to stop us or regulate us in any way.

Ken: I think we might be okay in that area. After all, we do all of our business in this state.

Jane: Yes, that's my point. All of our business is carried out in our home state. In fact, we even refine our own gasoline. That means we don't buy any gas from national oil companies for our delivery trucks.

Ken: Yes, and all the products that we use in our offices and labs are purchased in this state. Since we operate in only a single state, the federal government cannot touch us.

Jane: I hope you're right. Now about our patent application?

Lois: That's my job, Jane.

Jane: Any problems in that area, Lois?

Lois: Well, just one, but it's a big one.

Jane: What's the problem?

Lois: Well, our bacteria are living things and there is some question about whether they can be patented. I'm not sure what the requirements are or if a living thing will meet those requirements. So, I've got my team working on it.

Jane: Good. Now, I also want us to copyright that instruction booklet telling how to produce the bacteria, just in case we want to put that on the market too.

Sam: That's my job, Jane. We're okay on the booklet, but . . .

Jane: But what?

Sam: Well, the research and development team want to include some software with the booklet, and I'm not sure if we can copyright a computer program.

Jane: So what are you doing about it?

Sam: Well, I've got my team researching it right now. I think we can come up with an answer within a day or so.

Jane: Excellent. Now, I have just one more issue. I just received a report that there was a chemical spill during the production of a batch of the bacteria. What I want to know is if the Environmental Protection Agency can enforce its regulations against us.

Kris: Well, part of that answer will depend on whether the feds have any power over us at all.

Jane: Yes, that's true, but I don't want us to be caught unprepared. Let's just assume for the moment that somehow the feds have power over us.

Kris: Okay.

Jane: Then assuming this, I want to know if the EPA can fine us or make us clean up the river. I want to know all the implications of this situation.

Kris: I can handle that, Jane. I think we might be okay in this area. I don't think the EPA can touch us because the spill was accidental. But I'll check on it.

Jane: Okay. Now, does everyone know what has to be done?

All: Yes.

Jane: Okay. Let's get busy.

Memo — Patentability of UBCNA-52094

MEMORANDUM

To: Jane Johnson, President

From:

Date:

Subject: Patentability of UBCNA-52094

United Biotechnology Corporation of North America, Inc.

The Small Scale Scenarios

1. Betty Sherwood runs the Sherwood Florist, a small flower shop in the Kansas City Airport. Lately, Betty has been having problems paying her bills. Betty's daughter is in college and her mother is in an assisted living complex — both of whom she helps support. Betty has developed a plan to raise extra money. When customers come into the shop to place an order, she asks them if they are taking a trip. If they answer no, she charges them the normal rate because she assumes they are residents of Kansas City. The customer who answers yes is charged an additional 10 percent. Betty also asks where the customer lives. A 10 percent surcharge is added to the bills of New York City, Los Angeles, and Chicago residents because she believes they are used to paying higher prices. Is Betty's practice of charging certain customers more to help support her mother and daughter an ethical plan? Explain your answer.

2. Susan Miller recently started working after school at a local fast food restaurant. Her friend, Ryan Rogers, has worked at the same restaurant for about a year. After her first month, Susan discovers Ryan does not charge his friends for the food they order when they come into the restaurant after school. Susan tells Ryan that he should not give out free food. Instead of agreeing, Ryan tries to persuade Susan to do the same thing. Ryan argues that he only gives away food that will be thrown out because it has been on display too long. For awhile, Susan looks the other way and tells no one. Now, however, Ryan is giving away food hot off the grill. Moreover, he is also doing this on the weekends at breakfast and in the evening. Again, Susan tells Ryan he should stop giving food away. Ryan refuses. As a result, Susan decides to tell their supervisor. Ryan is then fired. Did Susan act ethically in telling the supervisor about Ryan? Explain.

3. Jerry Wolf has worked at the *Cleveland Plain Dealer* as a part-time news correspondent in the sports department for six years. His primary beat was professional football. When the Cleveland Browns left the city, Jerry found that his hours at the paper were cut considerably. His take home pay was about two-thirds of what it had been before the Browns left. Jerry is divorced and must meet his child support payments each month, as well as cover his own expenses. In order to make a bit more money, Jerry begins to pad his expense account every time he goes on an out-of-town assignment. At first, he charges for taxicab rides he did not take. He then figures out a system that allows him to use the computer to charge the newspaper for meals he did not eat, hotels he did not stay in, and plane tickets he did not purchase. Jerry believes this type of padding is "okay" because the paper owes it to him for his six years of loyal service. He is also concerned about his two children and wants to keep up-to-date on his child support payments. Has Jerry acted ethically? Explain.

4. Kelly Harris works at a clothing store at the Twin Oaks Mall. Max Stringer works for a music store in the same mall. Kelly and Max both get 20 percent discounts at their respective stores. The 20 percent discounts are also extended to the employee's immediate family. Kelly and Max have agreed to trade discounts. Kelly makes a list of new CDs for Max to purchase. Max complies and gives Kelly his discount. Max then goes shopping

at the clothing store. He gives Kelly a list of the clothes to purchase for him so he gets her discount. Since neither Kelly nor Max has any sisters or brothers, they believe trading discounts is "okay." Kelly is just taking the place of the sister Max does not have and vice versa. Therefore, no one is hurt and the trade-off is "okay." Have Kelly and Max acted ethically? Explain.

The Large Scale Scenarios

Northeastern Electronics and Communication Research and Exploration Corporation (NECREC pronounced "Neck-wreck") is a small, privately owned electronics firm located in the small town of Cedarville. The firm is the only major industry in town. It also employs most of the people in Cedarville, which is located in an economically depressed area of the state.

NECREC also provides the primary tax base for the town, including tax support for the school system and the local hospital. The local hospital has a newly built children's wing and a brand new nursing home facility, both of which will be paid for primarily by future taxes from NECREC.

The company does a marginal business supplying electronic component parts to airline companies and to the Department of Defense. However, it is on the verge of developing a new invention that will secure its financial future. To complete the project, the company must spend most of its reserve capital on the prototype.

THE COMPANY PRESIDENT

David Garvey, the head of the accounting department, approaches the president of the company, Lorraine Brooks, with some disturbing news. In reviewing the company books, Garvey has discovered that Brooks has been systematically overcharging the Department of Defense for the company's products. At times, the charges are 500 percent over cost and 900 percent over what the company charges private airlines for the same parts.

When confronted with this discrepancy, Brooks does not deny the overcharging. Rather, she defends it by saying the defense department can afford to pay the extra charges because it has such an outrageously high budget. Moreover, she reminds Garvey that the money the defense department spends is all tax revenue that comes from taxpayers. Since NECREC does more for the people of Cedarville than the defense department, she feels justified in the overcharges. Furthermore, she reminds Garvey that if he reveals the overcharging he will lose his job, the plant will shut down, jobs will be lost, and the economic base of the town will fall apart.

THE HEAD OF ACCOUNTING

Garvey returns to his office. He has been convinced by the president's arguments. However, he realizes he is walking a fine line and that someone else could discover the overcharging. Garvey has three children in college. His wife has been out of work for six months, and he is the sole support of his aging parents. Consequently, Garvey resolves that he needs something to protect himself and his family should the overcharging be discovered.

Since he is the head of accounting, it is not difficult to create several dummy accounts into which be begins to put company money. He does this systematically for three months. He has now accumulated a comfortable bank account of $100,000. Nevertheless, he continues to siphon money from the company treasury and put it into these private bank accounts. He reasons that, as the sole support of his wife, children, and parents, he has the right to protect himself with this money.

THE HEAD OF HUMAN RESOURCES

Brooks receives word that the defense department is going to audit the company's books. She responds by contacting her old friend, Nancy Chapman, head of the human resources department at the company. Chapman and Brooks have been friends and close confidants since high school. As a friend, Brooks confides in Chapman about the overcharging. She defends the overcharging in much the same way that she defended it to Garvey. Brooks then tells Chapman that the defense department is about to audit the books of the company. Consequently, she asks Chapman to write up a false report that will blame Garvey for the overcharging. In this way, Brooks will escape liability and can continue to run the company.

At first, Chapman refuses. Then Brooks tells her that Garvey has also been taking money from the firm for three months and has built up a sizable bank account from this money. Therefore, Brooks reasons he really is guilty of embezzlement and will be fired and prosecuted anyway. There is no need for both the president and the chief accountant to suffer. Chapman urges Brooks to tell the truth to the defense department and the company's board of directors. Brooks tells Chapman that she will think about it. Three days later, Brooks calls Chapman and says that she cannot tell the defense department or the board about her involvement in the overcharging. Chapman decides she must tell the board what is going on in the company.

THE OUTSIDE ATTORNEY

Michael Jameson is an attorney on the board of directors of NECREC. He is present when Chapman reports to the board about the overcharging by the president, the embezzlement by the head of accounting, and the upcoming defense department audit.

After the meeting, Jameson calls his old friend, Zachary Bishop, who is on the board of the United Communications Research Company. Jameson knows that Bishop owns several hundred thousand dollars of stock in NECREC. Jameson tells Bishop to sell his stock in NECREC immediately, while there is still time to make a profit.

Once the news of the overcharging, the embezzlement, and the impending audit becomes public knowledge, the price of NECREC stock will plummet. In exchange, Bishop tells Jameson that United Communications is planning a merger with Thompson Electronics. Consequently, if Jameson buys Thompson stock immediately, he will make a great deal of money. Both men comply with the suggestions, and both make a great deal of money in this exchange of information.

After reading the scenario, look at the piece of paper given to you by your teacher and determine which of the above named characters your group must examine. Then decide whether the actions taken by your character were ethical. Follow the suggested questions about your character given to you by your teacher. Once you have completed this task, if time allows, you may consider the ethical or unethical nature of the actions of the other characters.

Quantum Mechanical
Ethical Pledge of Conduct

WE, the owners and employees of Quantum Mechanical Industries, pledge . . .

- To be honest and straightforward with our customers at all times and on all matters.

- To be kind, courteous, and compassionate with our customers at all times and on all matters.

- To be fair, equitable, and just in our dealings with our customers at all times and on all matters.

- To treat our suppliers as we want to be treated when we are in the role of the supplier.

- To be prompt in service and deliveries to our customers and in payments to our suppliers.

- To stand up for what we believe in: our products, our services, and our dedication to be the best that we can be.

- To contribute to the development of a community spirit in and around the City of Cedarville.

- To support causes and campaigns that improve the quality of life in the City of Cedarville.

- To exceed the minimum standards of excellence within our industry.

- To treat each other with respect, courtesy, and honesty at all times and on all matters.

LESSON PLAN IX
BUSINESS PLANS

CHARACTERISTICS

MARKETING

ECONOMICS

FINANCE

ACCOUNTING

MANAGEMENT

GLOBAL MARKETS

LEGAL

BUSINESS PLANS

HANDOUTS

Business Plan Sections

Match the corresponding definition to each section of a business plan.

A. In order to secure financing, this section of the business plan must be as detailed as possible. Data to include consists of: sources of funding, start-up costs, break-even analysis, working capital requirements, past (if applicable) and projected income statements, balance sheet, and cash flow statement.

B. The entrepreneur must summarize the business plan by pointing out the assumptions and risks involved.

C. This section is critical to the development of a business plan because it focuses on the purpose of the business, the products and/or services offered, and the management philosophy that runs the business. This section also contains a vision statement, or what management expects to happen to the business in the future (short-term and long-term).

D. This section of the business plan indicates to bankers and potential investors that management has the ability to run the company successfully. A brief history detailing the qualifications of the owner(s) and key management personnel should be included, as well as their resumes. In addition, activities necessary to the running of the business (bookkeeping, employee hiring and firing, direct sales, customer relations, inventory control, purchasing, and so on) should be assigned to specific individuals.

E. This section of the business plan will be crucial because it describes how the business will compete in the marketplace. Topics include: a detailed description of the products and/or services to be offered, a profile of the customers to be targeted, pricing strategy, location description (advantages and disadvantages), and the promotional strategies to be utilized.

F. This section should provide an overview of the entire business plan and include only the essential facts. This section is important because, if not done well, the reader may not continue through the rest of the plan. While this section is placed at the beginning of the business plan, it will usually be the last section the preparer writes. It is possible that this part of the business plan can take the form of a cover letter, particularly when a business is applying for a loan.

G. National, industry, and local trends comprise the business environment and will affect whether a business can survive and grow. Some of the factors will include demographic changes, social trends, and legal requirements.

1. Executive Summary

   _____

2. Mission Statement

   _____

3. Business Environment

   _____

4. Management Team

5. Financial Data

6. Marketing Plan

7. Conclusion

Business Plan Sections (Answer Key)

INSTRUCTIONS

Match the corresponding definition to each section of a business plan.

A. Financial Data — In order to secure financing, this section of the business plan must be as detailed as possible. Data to include consists of: sources of funding, start-up costs, break-even analysis, working capital requirements, past (if applicable) and projected income statements, balance sheet, and cash flow statement.

B. Conclusion — The entrepreneur must summarize the business plan by pointing out the assumptions and risks involved.

C. Mission Statement — This section is critical to the development of a business plan because it focuses on the purpose of the business, the products and/or services offered, and the management philosophy that runs the business. This section also contains a vision statement, or what management expects to happen to the business in the future (short-term and long-term).

D. Management Team — This section of the business plan indicates to bankers and potential investors that management has the ability to run the company successfully. A brief history detailing the qualifications of the owner/s and key management personnel should be included, as well as their resumes. In addition, activities necessary to the running of the business (bookkeeping, employee hiring and firing, direct sales, customer relations, inventory control, purchasing, and so on) should be assigned to specific individuals.

E. Marketing Plan — This section of the business plan will be crucial because it describes how the business will compete in the marketplace. Topics include: a detailed description of the products and/or services to be offered, a profile of the customers to be targeted, pricing strategy, location description (advantages and disadvantages), and the promotional strategies to be utilized.

F. Executive Summary — This section should provide an overview of the entire business plan and include only the essential facts. This section is important because, if not done well, the reader may not continue through the rest of the plan. While this section is placed at the beginning of the business plan, it will usually be the last section the preparer writes. It is possible that this part of the business plan can take the form of a cover letter, particularly when a business is applying for a loan.

G. Business Environment — National, industry, and local trends comprise the business environment and will affect whether a business can survive and grow. Some of the factors will include demographic changes, social trends, and legal requirements.

1. Executive Summary

   F

2. Mission Statement

   C

3. Business Environment

   G

4. Management Team

    D

5. Financial Data

    A

6. Marketing Plan

    E

7. Conclusion

    B

Case Study — A Moneymaking Idea

INSTRUCTIONS

After reading the case, decide how Timothy and Tonya might answer the following questions about their plans for the refreshment stand. The answers to these questions should relate to specific sections of the business plan.

Timothy and Tonya are the 15-year old twin son and daughter of the Johnson family. Both children earn five dollars a week doing assigned tasks around their home. The twins would like a video game system that costs approximately $120 at the local discount store. Their parents say they must buy the system themselves. However, after general entertainment expenses, they never seem to have any money left to put toward the purchase. Mr. and Mrs. Johnson suggest the twins figure out a way to earn the money.

Summer vacation from school is approaching. Timothy and Tonya ponder the ways they could earn the money for the game system. They are aware that Mrs. Green is getting together items for the yard sale their neighborhood participates in twice a year (once at the beginning of the summer and once at the end). Remembering the large crowds that were present at last year's sales and the unbearable heat, the twins come up with a business idea. Why not fill a large cooler with ice, cans of soft drinks, and candy bars and sell these to the customers of the neighborhood sale? "And remember," Tonya tells her brother, "we would have to clear only $60 at each yard sale in order to be able to buy the system."

Mr. and Mrs. Johnson like the children's entrepreneurial spirit and might be willing to help with a loan to buy the initial product (soft drinks, candy bars) for the venture. The Johnsons agree that the twins can borrow their large picnic cooler and be-

gin making ice and storing it in the freezer in the basement. This would save on overhead costs.

The family decides on a business meeting to consider the proposal. Mr. Johnson is a loan officer at the local bank, and he insists that the twins be prepared to answer any questions about their business venture. The Johnsons are members of a local warehouse club, and soft drinks are selling for $.20 a 12-ounce can and candy bars for $.15 each.

1. How should the twins present their overall moneymaking idea to their parents?

_____

_____

_____

_____

_____

2. What do the twins plan beyond this summer's sales? Will they try to repeat the venture next year? If they make more than the required $120, do the twins have any plans for the excess income?

_____

_____

_____

_____

_____

3. Do the twins foresee any potential problems on the day of the yard sale?

_____

_____

_____

_____

_____

4. Do the twins have a plan to assign specific duties on the days of the sales? How will these duties be assigned?

_____

_____

_____

_____

_____

5. How do the twins determine how much to charge for each item? How many cans of soft drinks and how many candy bars do the twins need to sell to reach their goal?

_____

_____

_____

_____

_____

6. How do the twins determine how much product (soft drinks, candy bars, etc.) to buy? What kind of soft drinks and candy would be popular (diet, non-caffeine, etc.)? How do the twins plan to make the participants in the yard sale aware of their products?

_____

_____

_____

_____

_____

Case Study — A Moneymaking Idea (Answer Key)

INSTRUCTIONS

After reading the case, decide how Timothy and Tonya might answer the following questions about their plans for the refreshment stand. The answers to these questions should relate to specific sections of the business plan.

Timothy and Tonya are the 15-year old twin son and daughter of the Johnson family. Both children earn five dollars a week doing assigned tasks around their home. The twins would like a video game system that costs approximately $120 at the local discount store. Their parents say they must buy the system themselves. However, after general entertainment expenses, they never seem to have any money left to put toward the purchase. Mr. and Mrs. Johnson suggest the twins figure out a way to earn the money.

Summer vacation from school is approaching. Timothy and Tonya ponder the ways they could earn the money for the game system. They are aware that Mrs. Green is getting together items for the yard sale their neighborhood participates in twice a year (once at the beginning of the summer and once at the end). Remembering the large crowds that were present at last year's sales and the unbearable heat, the twins come up with a business idea. Why not fill a large cooler with ice, cans of soft drinks, and candy bars and sell these to the customers of the neighborhood sale? "And remember," Tonya tells her brother, "we would have to clear only $60 at each yard sale in order to be able to buy the system."

Mr. and Mrs. Johnson like the children's entrepreneurial spirit and might be willing to help with a loan to buy the initial product (soft drinks, candy bars) for the venture. The Johnsons agree that the twins can borrow their large picnic cooler and begin making ice and storing it in the freezer in the basement. This would save on overhead costs.

The family decides on a business meeting to consider the proposal. Mr. Johnson is a loan officer at the local bank, and he insists that the twins be prepared to answer any questions about their business venture. The Johnsons are members of a local warehouse club, and soft drinks are selling for $.20 a 12-ounce can and candy bars for $.15 each.

1. How should the twins present their overall moneymaking idea to their parents?

   [Executive Summary] — The twins should be organized before meeting with their parents. They should schedule a specific time for the business meeting and explain their intentions for earning the money for the video game system. If the twins need to borrow money from their parents for this venture, this should also be part of the meeting.

2. What do the twins plan beyond this summer's sales? Will they try to repeat the venture next year? If they make more than the required $120, do the twins have any plans for the excess income?

   [Mission Statement] — The twins should understand that money is often the cause of arguments; they should decide at the beginning what will become of any extra income. Probably an even split would be appropriate, but they might total hours worked and decide to split the income proportionately. The twins should decide what level of success would tempt them to try the venture again next year.

3. Do the twins foresee any potential problems on the day of the yard sale?

[Business Environment] — The twins should foresee problems: buyers unaware of their refreshment stand, location too far away to be accessible to everyone, rain, running out of product, insufficient change, ice melting too fast, local ordinances prohibiting selling in certain locations, other people with the same business idea (competition), etc.

4. Do the twins have a plan to assign specific duties on the days of the sales? How will these duties be assigned?

[Management Team] — One twin should be responsible for sales (selling products, making change, taking care of cash, being polite to customers). The other twin should be responsible for inventory (making sure cooler has sufficient ice, enough pop and candy on hand to satisfy customers, general maintenance of selling area).

5. How do the twins determine how much to charge for each item? How many cans of soft drinks and how many candy bars do the twins need to sell to reach their goal?

[Financial Data] — The twins should plug different prices into the equation in order to see the effect on their total profit. Since they plan to sell at both yard sales, the twins need only $60 each time. It should be noted that their prices should be competitive with comparable businesses in the area.

(Price of Candy Bars - Cost of Candy Bars) x Estimated Units Sold = Gross Profit

(Price of Soft Drinks - Cost of Soft Drinks) x Estimated Units Sold = Gross Profit

_____

TOTAL PROFIT

6. How do the twins determine how much product (soft drinks, candy bars, etc.) to buy? What kind of soft drinks and candy would be popular (diet, non-caffeine, etc.)? How do the twins plan to make the participants in the yard sale aware of their products?

[Marketing Plan] — The twins should do basic market research, such as asking neighbors the approximate number of people attending last year's sale. At the same time, they should ask the adults what soft drinks and candy bars would be popular with everyone (including children). Then they should use this information to estimate stock needs. The twins should brainstorm advertising ideas: a large sign near their cooler, flyers at each yard sale house, requesting neighbors to put "REFRESHMENTS AVAILABLE" on their signs, and so on.

Business Plan Sections

1. Executive Summary — This section should provide an overview of the entire business plan and include only the essential facts. This section is important because, if not done well, the reader may not continue through the rest of the plan. While this section is placed at the beginning of the business plan, it will usually be the last section the preparer writes. It is possible that this part of the business plan can take the form of a cover letter, particularly when a business is applying for a loan.

2. Mission Statement — This section is critical to the development of a business plan because it focuses on the purpose of the business, the products and/or services offered, and the management philosophy that runs the business. This section also contains a vision statement, or what management expects to happen to the business in the future (short-term and long-term).

3. Business Environment — National, industry, and local trends comprise the business environment and will affect whether a business can survive and grow. Some of the factors will include demographic changes, social trends, and legal requirements.

4. Management Team — This section of the business plan indicates to bankers and potential investors that management has the ability to run the company successfully. A brief history detailing the qualifications of the owner(s) and key management personnel should be included, as well as their resumes. In addition, activities necessary to the running of the business (bookkeeping, employee hiring and firing, direct sales, customer relations, inventory control, purchasing, and so on) should be assigned to specific individuals.

5. Financial Data — In order to secure financing, this section of the business plan must be as detailed as possible. Data to include consists of: sources of funding, start-up costs, break-even analysis, working capital requirements, past (if applicable) and projected income statements, balance sheet, and cash flow statement.

6. Marketing Plan — This section of the business plan will be crucial. Here you will describe how your business will compete in the marketplace. Topics include: a detailed description of the products and/or services to be offered, a profile of the customers to be targeted, pricing strategy, location description (advantages and disadvantages), and the promotional strategies to be utilized.

7. Conclusion — The entrepreneur must summarize the business plan by pointing out the assumptions and risks involved.

Case Study — Sarah's Speedy Service

INSTRUCTIONS

Read the following case study and record important information under the appropriate section of the business plan.

When Sarah was in high school, she noticed that a number of her classmates rented limousines for the junior/senior prom. She knew the rides were pretty expensive, but the people she talked to didn't seem to mind. It was a special occasion, and they said it was worth it for just one night.

Sarah asked her parents about the limousine business. They told her that limousines were also rented for weddings, anniversaries, group trips, and other special occasions. Later, during her college years, Sarah noticed that her classmates rented limousines to go to out-of-town football games, formal dance occasions, graduation, and other events.

For a graduation present, Sarah's grandparents gave her a lump sum of money. She had not forgotten her observations on the limousine business (and by now she knew that she was crazy about driving), and she used the money to buy a used limousine.

The business started slowly. Initially, Sarah worked out of her parents' home. However, she decided that was unprofessional, and rented a small storefront in the downtown area. She had her own business telephone line, voice mail service, charge card privileges, uniforms, and her business name printed on the front window.

Sarah did little or no advertising. She had business cards printed and used these as a way to get her name in front of the public. A college profes-sor had told her that word-of-mouth was the best form of advertising, so Sarah just figured it would take a while for anyone to know she was open for business.

Two years later, Sarah's business is very success-ful. She has regular clients, and her income has steadied to the point where she believes another limousine would increase her revenue dramati-cally. She has come to you for advice on obtain-ing a business loan. That same college professor told her that a business plan was absolutely nec-essary if she was to seek financing. Sarah says she has no experience in formulating a business plan, but if you would be willing to help, she would give you and your friends 10 free rides over the next year.

Gross Revenue	Year 1	Year 2
June	$ 450	$2,600
July	$ 625	$2,700
August	$ 900	$2,860
September	$1,000	$3,450
October	$1,050	$2,845
November	$1,350	$2,650
December	$1,800	$4,200
January	$1,900	$3,560
February	$1,200	$2,940
March	$2,100	$2,450
April	$2,350	$3,635
May	$3,200	$4,975

Current Monthly Expenses	
Rent	$ 350
Utilities	$ 125
Telephone	$ 215
Dry Cleaning	$ 65
Supplies	$ 40
Printing	$ 40
Amenities (Roses, Etc.)	$ 165
Gasoline	$ 650
Insurance	$ 350
Salary (Sarah)	$1,500

This is the financial information supplied by Sarah:
    Cash in bank: $875
    Current value of limousine (estimate): $14,000
    Lease on storefront: Five-year option for five more years at $450 per month.

Sarah likes her business a great deal. She is personable, and the customers like her. She offers little amenities like a rose for the females, a key chain for the males, refreshments during the trip, and the music that the customers request.

Sarah knows that buying another limousine would mean she would have to hire another driver. This scares her because she does not know if she will be able to train someone to do the job as well as she does. Sarah knows it is easier to work hard in your own business than it is to work for someone else.

There is one other limousine service in town, but it specializes in weddings and doesn't handle the other events that Sarah specializes in. She doesn't know exactly, but figures her gross revenue will increase by 50-60 percent with another car. Of course, the expenses will go up accordingly.

The limousine is in good shape (Sarah keeps regular maintenance) but will need some repairs in the next year to remain in top running condition.

Sarah has talked to a local loan officer, and she can use her current limousine as collateral for a loan. The bank would hold the title to her current limousine and the title to the new one. The monthly payments would be approximately $425 for seven years.

1. Executive Summary

_____

_____

_____

_____

_____

_____

2. Mission Statement

_____

_____

_____

_____

_____

_____

3. Business Environment

_____

_____

_____

_____

4. Management Team

_____

_____

_____

_____

_____

5. Financial Data

_____

_____

_____

_____

_____

6. Marketing Plan

_____

_____

_____

_____

_____

7. Conclusion

_____

_____

_____

_____

_____

Your Business Plan Outline

1. Executive Summary — List basic, important facts that will convince the reader to look at the remainder of the business plan.

_____

_____

_____

_____

2. Mission Statement — What is the purpose of your business? What products and/or services do you plan to provide? What is your management philosophy of running a small business?

_____

_____

_____

_____

3. Business Environment — What local, industry, and national trends might affect your business? Is the population changing in your area? Is your product environmentally safe? Will health-conscious people want your product?

_____

_____

_____

_____

_____

4. Management Team — Who will run the daily operations of your business? What skills does each individual bring to the business? What experience does each person have in this particular or related industry? How will the working hours be split up?

_____

_____

_____

_____

5. Financial Data — Where will your start-up capital come from? How much do you plan to invest in the business? What income do you predict from your operations for the first year? Second year? First five years? How much collateral do you have?

_____

_____

_____

_____

6. **Marketing Plan** — What type of advertising do you plan to use? What media will be the best for your business? What is the description of your target market? Have you chosen a location? What are the advantages and disadvantages of your location choice? What day-to-day promotions do you plan to use to market your business?

_____

_____

_____

_____

_____

7. **Conclusion** — What assumptions have you made about this business that may not turn out exactly right? What risks are involved in this business?

_____

_____

_____

_____

_____